# 853 HARD
# TO BELIEVE
# FACTS

by

Nayden Kostov

# 853 HARD TO BELIEVE FACTS

by

Nayden Kostov

Luxembourg
2018

# 853 HARD TO BELIEVE FACTS
first edition

| | |
|---|---|
| Author: | Nayden Kostov |
| Editors: | Jonathon Tabet and Andrea Leitenberger |
| Format: | 5,25 x 8 |

ISBN:       978-99959-980-7-3

# CONTENTS

**6**

# PROLOGUE

This book is full of fun and verified facts, presented in an accessible manner that I hope will provide you with hours of entertainment. My objective has been to provide you with a lifetime supply of icebreakers and points of discussion. Amaze your friends and family by telling them that pistachios can combust spontaneously or that the holes in pen caps are there to save people from choking to death!

Following the success of my site RaiseYourBrain.com, I decided to collect the best trivia gems and present you with a fact compendium suitable for a wide audience. This is the product of years of sifting through history and references books on a myriad of subjects as well as searching the Internet and paying attention to the news. In 2016, I published "1123 Hard to Believe Facts", which was read by tens of thousands and accumulated hundreds of 5-star reviews on Amazon and GoodReads. As it has remained in the Top 10 of its category for almost two years now, I decided that another instalment was merited, this time with more illustrations and detailed explanations.

This book is suitable for most audiences across the age spectrum. The "spiciest" entries are neatly separated in the chapter "Facts about human and animal sexuality". They remain factual and abstain from profanity. To my greatest delight, an avid reader of my website explained that he was preparing daily fact sheets for his son's lunch box. He prints out three facts every day to create some lunchtime fun for his child in the hope of sparking intellectual curiosity. I honestly wish my parents had done the same for me when I was a lad!

# CHAPTER I

*Unbelievable facts about virtually everything*

### 1.

It is technically possible to be born more than once. A baby was "born" twice in Texas, USA, in 2016 after she was taken out of her mother's uterus for twenty minutes in order for the surgeons to perform life-saving surgery.

### 2.

The video game Tetris was first released in the Soviet Union in 1984. It appeared in the West a year later.

### 3.

Nutella was invented during WWII because there was a shortage of chocolate. As its name suggests, it contains more hazelnuts than cocoa. As an aside, the producing company Ferrero uses 25% of the global supply of hazelnuts.

### 4.

In 1908, the Russian Olympic team arrived in London, UK, twelve days late because they were still using the Julian calendar. The Russian Orthodox Church still follows it, which is why Christmas in Russia falls on 7 January rather than on 25 December.

### 5.

Jupiter is the fastest rotating planet in the Solar System.

6.

During the 1948 US Presidential Election, everyone was so sure Thomas Dewey would be elected the next US President that the Chicago Daily Tribune put a "Dewey Defeats Truman" front-pager before the final results were announced. Truman eventually won and proudly posed with the newspaper.

7.

Trees in the rainforest grow year-round and therefore have no rings.

8.

Ants have the highest brain to body size ratio of any animal.

9.

In many countries in Central and Eastern Europe (Bulgaria, Czech Republic, Romania, Russia, Ukraine, etc.) men never give an even number of flowers to a lady. Even numbers bouquets are reserved for funerals.

10.

Native tribes in Central America invented wheeled toys thousands of years ago. By the time America was colonised, however, they had not yet found a practical use for the wheel.

11.

A bird's beak grows constantly, just like human nails. Natural wear and tear however keeps the beak's size more or less constant.

### 12.
Panophobia means "fear of everything".

### 13.
A woman from Perth, Australia, is able to smell Parkinson's disease before patients show any symptoms.

### 14.
Belize is the only English-speaking country in Central America.

### 15.
Celluloid billiard balls can literally explode on impact.

### 16.
Most Dutch people believe that reheating spinach is very dangerous and can lead to poisoning although there is little scientific evidence supporting this.

### 17.
White candy cotton is 100% sugar.

### 18.
Table tennis (aka ping-pong) was prohibited in the Soviet Union for quite some time (1930 - 1950) as it was thought to damage eyesight.

19.

Out of superstition, the Japanese avoid whistling or cutting their nails after dark. Whistling was historically associated with burglars signalling to each other at night, while cutting your nails is thought to "summon evil spirits".

20.

The billionaire and founder of Alibaba Corporation, Jack Ma, is worth almost USD 40 billion (2017 data). Before finding success as an entrepreneur, he unsuccessfully applied ten times to Harvard University, and even was once turned down for a job at Kentucky Fried Chicken.

21.

Julius Wagner-Jauregg received a Nobel Prize in 1927 for his discovery that if one had syphilis and then contracted malaria, the high fever would cure the syphilis.

22.

The Hague is the third biggest inhabited locality in the Netherlands with its 510,000 citizens. Administratively speaking however, it has never received an official city status and is therefore dubbed "the largest village in Europe".

23.

In a freezer, a cup of hot water without a lid sometimes freezes faster than an identical cup of cold water. This is referred to as the Mpemba effect, named after Erasto Mpemba, a 13-year old Tanzanian student who discovered it while making ice cream.

24.

Initially, battle tanks were categorised into "male" and "female" tanks based on their main armament. Male tanks were equipped with cannons, while females had heavy machine guns.

25.

During WWI, France built a "fake Paris" near the real city in order to confuse German pilots.

26.

100,000 tons of chewing gum are produced each year.

27.

As a young soldier, Hitler used to have a normal-sized moustache, but he was ordered to trim it down in order to better accommodate a gas mask.

28.

Because they contain "hidden non-edible pieces", Kinder Surprise chocolate eggs are outlawed in the USA in their original form.

29.

Japanese eat Kentucky Fried Chicken (KFC) for Christmas. It all started in 1974 when KFC Japan successfully promoted fried chicken as a Christmas meal.

30.

The founder of KFC, Colonel Sanders, practiced law without a law degree and delivered babies without a medical degree.

31.

The book "Everything men know about women" has 120 blank pages. It has sold over a million copies so far.

32.

The South Korean automotive brand Hyundai carried out a public crash test to prove that their cars are equally safe regardless of the country they are produced in.

33.

Bulgaria had more military airplanes than the USA until 1912. Bulgarian air force was the first to drop bombs from an airplane.

34.

The word "democracy" is not found in the Constitution of the USA nor is it present in the Declaration of Independence.

35.

Adolf Hitler objected to the use of poison gas on the battlefield in WWII partly because he had been gassed as a soldier during WWI.

36.

Peanuts used to be a key ingredient in dynamite.

### 37.

Birmingham, United Kingdom, is often referred to as the city of 1,000 inventions. About 70% of all inventions copyrighted in the UK came from within a 50-km (35-mi) radius of the city.

### 38.

Okay, OK, refers to an actual town in Oklahoma, USA.

### 39.

The closest distance between Russia and the United States of America is only 4 km (2.5 mi), between the islands Little Diomede (USA) and Big Diomede (Russia).

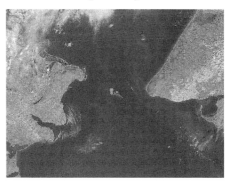

### 40.

The congested traffic in Moscow, Russia, has led some wealthy Russians to hire fake ambulances to beat the jams.

41.

Saint Joseph of Cupertino is the patron saint
of astronauts.

42.

Oceans cover 70% of Earth's surface. Yet, rather
counterintuitively, lightning is more likely to strike
land surface than water.

43.

Mount Everest (in the Himalayas) was formed
millions of years after the Tyrannosaurus rex
became extinct.

44.

In 2008, a Canadian man replaced his fake eye with a
bionic camera.

45.

Walt Disney was the first to use the marketing
approach called "synergy".

46.

The first hybrid car was built one century earlier than
you probably think. The first design under the name
"System Lohner-Porsche" was patented in 1898.

47.

In Japan, ladies cover their mouths when laughing because it is considered rude to show one's teeth.

48.

In 1989, the USSR gave Pepsico seventeen submarines, a cruiser, a frigate, and a destroyer in exchange for Pepsi products.

49.

Etorphine is 3,000 times stronger than morphine. Less than 15 mg of it is enough to immobilise an African elephant.

50.

Ostriches have the smallest eggs relative to size in the animal kingdom. Although being the largest single cell in nature, an ostrich egg is less than 1.5% of the mother's weight.

51.

Ostriches need to raise their head in order to swallow when eating and drinking.

52.

Young ostriches grow at a rate of 1 cm (half an inch) per day.

## 53.

Norwegians use the word "Texas" as
a synonym for "crazy".

## 54.

New Zealand's capital, Wellington, is
the world's southernmost.

## 55.

In Japan, you should never place your chopsticks
upright in your rice as such action is part of
a funeral ceremony.

## 56.

In Japan, many people hide their thumbs from hearses
(funeral vehicles) and when passing close to a
graveyard. They say that "your parents will die young
if you do not hide your thumbs". This is linked to the
fact that the Japanese word for "thumb" translates
into "parent finger".

## 57.

Taste tester of pet food is an actual job.

## 58.

Across the majority of the Western nations, the higher
the average wedding costs, the higher the probability
of divorce.

59.

The Romanian gymnast Nadia Comaneci became the first athlete ever to receive the maximal 10.00 score at the Olympic Games in Montreal, Canada, in 1976.

60.

About 1% of all insects are ants.

61.

Barbie doll's full name is Barbara Millicent "Barbie" Roberts.

62.

Twelve publishing houses rejected J. K. Rowling's Harry Potter before it got published. William Golding's "Lord of the Flies" was rejected twenty times.

63.

Pheasants are the birds with the longest feathers.

64.

The first Barbie doll was sold in 1959.

65.

Theophilus Van Kannel patented the world's first revolving door in 1888. He had a phobia of opening doors for others, especially for women.

### 66.

Milunka Savic is a Serbian war hero. She took the place of her brother as the army mobilised and fought in the Balkan Wars and WWI. By the time her real gender was discovered, she had already been decorated and promoted to corporal.

### 67.

Scuba divers cannot fart at depths of more than 10 m (33 ft).

### 68.

Cabernet Sauvignon is the most consumed type of red wine worldwide.

### 69.

When Marco Polo first saw rhinos, he thought they were unicorns.

### 70.

In the Greek language, "symposium" roughly means "drinking together".

### 71.

The earliest copy of the masterpiece Mona Lisa was painted by one of Leonardo da Vinci's students. It is presently kept in the Prado Museum in Madrid, Spain.

**72.**

The zone that controls the eyes, the occipital lobe, covers almost one quarter of the entire human brain.

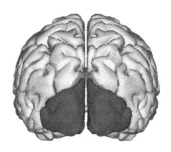

**73.**

China has grown more maize (corn) than rice since 2011.

**74.**

Jelly bears are quite effective in stopping bullets.

**75.**

Since 2016 and as of writing, one salmon fish costs more than a barrel of oil.

**76.**

There are almost 2,000 species of fleas.

### 77.

In 2015, top Chinese actress and model Angelababy had her face examined to prove she had not undergone plastic surgery.

### 78.

After the Fukushima earthquake, the islands of Japan moved sideways by 2.5 m (8 ft) and Earth tilted by 18 cm (7 in).

### 79.

The budget of the movie "Titanic" (1997) was in fact larger than the cost of building the actual ship.

### 80.

The metric system was introduced in 1875. Today, only three countries have not yet officially adopted it: the USA, Liberia and Myanmar.

81.

The US Congress's Metric Conversion Act, passed in 1975, declared that "the metric system is the preferred system of weights and measures for US trade and commerce" and established the United States Metric Board. President Ronald Reagan however abolished the Metric Board in 1982, ensuring continued use of imperial measurements in the USA.

82.

Photoshop prevents you from working on full-size pictures of real banknotes.

83.

Catholics were barred from becoming teachers, doctors or nurses in Sweden until 1951.

84.

An 85-year-old Austrian woman singlehandedly shredded almost one million euro in banknotes. She wanted to annoy her relatives one more time before dying.

85.

The melody of the national anthem of the United Kingdom, "God Save the Queen", is also used for the national anthem of Liechtenstein, "Oben am jungen Rhein" ("Up above the Young Rhine").

### 86.

Female badgers can delay the implantation of embryos in their uterus for months in order to time birth for a more favourable season.

### 87.

Killing or harming a badger is an offence in England and can lead to six months in prison.

### 88.

In the period between 1850 and 1916, all soldiers in the British Army were required to sport moustaches.

### 89.

Genetically modified salmon has already been approved for sale by the US Food and Drug Administration.

### 90.

The world's longest standing alliance was ratified in 1386 CE and is still in force. It is between the United Kingdom and Portugal.

### 91.

Madison was barely used as a girl's name before 1985. It however became the second-most-popular name given to baby girls in the USA in 2001. The rise in its popularity is attributed to the movie "Splash" (1984).

### 92.

According to the ancient Israeli Sanhedrin court system, a suspect cannot be sentenced if all twenty-three members of the jury agreed on his or her guilt. This rule was thought to prevent biased verdicts.

### 93.

Cockroaches run at top speed of 1 m/s (3 ft/s).

### 94.

As of 2017, half of the new cars registered in Norway are either electric or hybrid.

### 95.

The holes in pen caps are there to save people from choking to death.

### 96.

Bundanoon, Australia, became the first town in the world to outlaw bottled water in 2009. Many other cities followed suit, the largest being San Francisco, USA, which banned plastic water bottles in 2014.

### 97.

Thomas Edison, the famous inventor, was considered "addled" by his schoolmaster. Edison's mother (a teacher by training) took him out of school at age of eight and home-schooled him.

98.

Miniature elephants used to live around the Mediterranean Sea. The discovery of their fossilised skulls in antiquity may have given birth to the myths of the cyclops.

99.

Playing the didgeridoo (a wind instrument developed by Indigenous Australians of northern Australia) relieves stress, reduces snoring and improves blood circulation.

100.

A queen termite is 100 times larger than other termites.

101.

Soldiers and workers termites can be either male or female whereas soldier and worker bees and ants are almost always exclusively female.

102.

Termite mounds in Australia are the tallest non-man-made constructions.

103.

A 2HB pencil can draw a continuous line of roughly 55 km (35 mi).

## 104.

In the course of the last 150 years, Russia has been ruled alternately by hairy and bald rulers. Georgy Malenkov who succeeded Stalin has been the only exception so far. Based on this historic trend, we should expect Putin's successor to be hairy!

## 105.

There are insects named after Robert Redford, Che Guevara, Darth Vader, Kate Winslet, Liv Tyler, Adolf Hitler, and Arnold Schwarzenegger.

## 106.

The coconut crab literally climbs trees to pick up coconuts. It has also been observed attacking nesting birds.

### 107.

Some shopping centres and restaurants play classical music in their car parks at night to stop teenagers from gathering there.

### 108.

In the USA, only the US Congress can declare a war. This power is not shared with anyone, including the President. Approximately half of the Americans are unaware of this fact.

### 109.

Each astronaut on the International Space Station can only take with them 1.5 kg (3 pounds) of personal effects.

### 110.

Coca-Cola was invented by Dr. John S. Pemberton as an alternative to alcoholic beverages. Ironically, his decision to sell the business was partly driven by his expensive morphine addiction.

### 111.

Violet Jessop, dubbed "Miss Unsinkable", survived the sinking of the sister ships the Titanic and the Britannic, and was also aboard the Olympic when it had a major accident.

## 112.

14% of the world population do not have the wrist muscle called "Palmaris longus".

## 113.

In case you wondered, Easter Island figures (called *moai*) do have bodies. The tallest moai erected measured almost 10 m (33 ft) high and weighed 82 tonnes (90.4 tons).

## 114.

Laura Hall became the first person to be banned from drinking in an entire country (actually, in two countries: England and Wales) in 2010.

## 115.

Chinese steel production increased twelvefold in the period 1990-2015.

## 116.

The smallest town in the world is Hum, Croatia. It has only 30 inhabitants but has preserved its town institutions from the time when its population was considerably larger.

## 117.

Slinky, the toy that can travel down a flight of steps end-over-end, was invented in 1943.

## 118.

The streets of Chesham's town centre (UK) feature Smart Wi-Fi Pavements, providing free internet since 2015.

## 119.

1954 was the year when the most numerous sightings of the Virgin Mary were reported.

## 120.

Haiti became the first independent "black" state in the New World in 1804.

## 121.

Languages originating in warm areas with a dense tree cover tend to use fewer consonants.

122.

Baby rabbits are referred to as "kittens".

123.

Almonds belong to the peach family.

124.

The term "mulatto" did not vanish entirely from the US census until 1930.

125.

New-born bear cubs weigh on average 300 g (0.7 pound). Their weight increases by a factor of 200 in the course of their first year.

### 126.
Habitually, male gorillas sleep on the ground in a nest made from leaves and twigs, while most females and babies nest in trees.

### 127.
The Japanese company Yamaha has developed a robot capable of riding a motorbike.

### 128.
Chicken tikka masala was not invented in India. The dish originated in Glasgow, Scotland.

### 129.
The town of Lauscher, Germany, produced the entire world's supply of Christmas balls between 1840 and 1940.

### 130.
In 2015, Bugatti (a car brand presently owned by Volkswagen) released a model that changes its colour.

### 131.
-40 degrees Fahrenheit and -40 degrees Celsius is exactly the same temperature.

## 132.
Good news for the vegans: the Irish beer brand Guinness will no longer contain traces of fish bladder, previously an ingredient used during its filtration process.

## 133.
The *axolotl*, although colloquially known as a "walking fish", is actually an amphibian.

## 134.
Bees are very sensitive to magnetism. They also use the Sun for orientation and are even able to detect its position at night.

## 135.
Honeybees can recognise human faces.

## 136.
Some amphibious animals use their nostrils to smell and not to breathe.

## 137.
The worse a pregnant woman experiences morning sickness, the smaller the chance of a stillbirth.

### 138.

According to the Guinness Book of World Records, the largest kite which has ever flown has a total lifting area of 950 m² (10,225 sq ft). It represents a huge Kuwait flag and flew for the first time in 2005.

### 139.

No single case of schizophrenia has ever been reported among people born blind or having lost their eyesight as infants.

### 140.

A Eucalyptus tree can grow as much as 10 metres in a year. As of early 2018, the tallest measured specimen is 100 m (327 ft) tall.

## 141.
Eucalyptus oil is highly flammable, which means that gum trees literally explode in bushfires.

## 142.
The male Australian lyrebird can imitate the calls of at least twenty other birds. He can also perfectly mimic sounds such as that of a chainsaw and a car alarm.

## 143.
Banana plants can move sideways up to 40 centimetres (more than one foot) in a lifetime.

## 144.
*Feng shui* sprang from the art of choosing an appropriate place for a grave.

## 145.
Koalas almost never drink water. Their name actually means "no water" in several aboriginal languages of Australia.

## 146.
Theoretically, we can "breathe" a liquid enriched with 40% oxygen. Tests with mice in the 1960s were quite promising but no successful experiment with people has yet been reported.

147.

Alan Smithee is the fictional name given to a director who disowns his own movie.

148.

The French poodle dog breed in fact originated in Germany.

149.

Hawaii is the only US state without a straight line on its borders. It is also the only one to use the United Kingdom's Union Jack on its flag.

150.

Alexander the Great introduced sugar, bananas, cotton and crucifixion to Europe.

### 151.
Skin accounts for a quarter of a
hippopotamus's weight.

### 152.
Hippos usually breastfeed under water. Their milk is
coloured a bright pink.

### 153.
Sometimes wallabies get high after breaking into
opium crops, then run around in a frenzy and make
what look like crop circles.

### 154.
Alligators change up to 3,000 teeth in their lifetime.

### 155.
The male platypus's venom can kill a dog. Luckily, the
platypus is not an aggressive animal and uses the
venomous spurs exclusively for self-defence.

### 156.
A US environmentalist, John Francis, voluntarily spent
seventeen years without talking (from 1973 until
1990). Whilst under his vow of silence, he completed
three college degrees as well as a PhD.

157.
Pigeons are the only bird that can suck up water.

158.
In computer animation, 1/100 of a second is called a "jiffy".

159.
At birth, a kangaroo is only one centimetre long (half an inch).

160.

If a kangaroo is chased by a dog close to a lake or river, it may jump into the water for safety. If followed there, the kangaroo will typically try to drown the dog.

161.

Kangaroos are capable of living for several months without drinking a drop of water. Should they desperately need some, kangaroos dig "wells" over 1 m (4 ft) deep.

162.

The fox has the largest habitat among all carnivorous mammals on land.

163.

On the island of La Gomera (one of the Canary Islands, Spain), the traditional whistling language "*silbo gomero*" is taught at school.

164.

In early 2016, a 150-year-old mousetrap caught a mouse in a UK museum. The trap was a part of the exhibition and was not considered to be operational.

165.

Leeches have thirty-two brains.

166.

Reindeer have 1,500 hairs per cm$^2$ (over 10,000 per sq in). These insulate very efficiently and help them survive extremely low temperatures.

167.

Paper comes to printing houses on huge rolls. A single roll can weigh over a ton and have more than 21 km (13 mi) of paper on it.

168.

Grey whales travel a distance equal to half the length of the equator every year.

169.

Macaques never eat an entire fruit if there is another fruit available nearby.

170.

Cockatoos sometimes eat so much that they lose the ability to fly for a certain period.

171.

Hillary Clinton won a Grammy Award in 1997. Her audiobook "It Takes a Village: And Other Lessons Children Teach Us" won in the category Best Spoken Word or Non-Musical Album.

172.

During her freshman year at Wellesley College in 1965, Hillary Clinton served as the president of the Young Republicans.

173.

Madrid, Spain, is farther north from the equator than Washington DC, USA.

174.

In the 1960s, during the Cold War, the USA and the Soviet Union tried to create nuclear-powered bombers. Both research programs were scrapped before an operational aircraft could be constructed.

175.

On the International Space Station, Sunday is a day of rest.

176.

The assault rifle, AK-47, appears on the flag of Mozambique and on the coats of arms of Zimbabwe, Burkina Faso (even though only from 1984 to 1997) and East Timor. The rifle is also seen on the flags of the Lebanese militant organisation Hezbollah and the Revolutionary Guard of the Islamic Republic of Iran.

177.

The former US President, Barack Obama, left his successor with 11 million followers on Twitter. As of early 2018, Donald Trump has around 20 million.

178.

Amidst the 2016 US presidential race, a guest at a Donald Trump hotel requested a framed photo of Hillary Clinton. Hotel staff duly delivered it.

179.

Ironically enough, the very same lawyers whom Donald Trump had hired to defend him from the lawsuits by unpaid employees, proceeded to sue him for unpaid bills in 2016.

180.

Torpedoes have two propellers turning in opposite directions.

181.

The Nile catfish swims upside down.

182.

Every Halloween, people in the USA spend more than two billion dollars on candy.

183.

The automotive brand Rolls Royce offers cars in 44,000 colours.

184.

All mammals, except for sloths and manatees, have seven neck vertebrae.

185.

The nine species of moa were the only wingless (do not mistake with "flightless") birds that ever existed on Earth. They used to inhabit New Zealand and were overhunted to extinction around 1500 CE by the Maori.

186.

In the period 1941 - 1945, hamburgers in the USA were re-named "Liberty Steaks" to get rid of the German-sounding name.

187.

On the Faroe Islands, they fit cameras on the back of sheep to create Google Street View.

188.

Diocletian was the only Roman emperor to abdicate voluntarily.

189.

Jehovah's Witnesses is one of the few religions that have never been involved in a war. Its followers do not use the cross and do not accept blood transfusions.

190.

10 kg (22.5 pounds) of eggplant contain the nicotine equivalent to one cigarette.

### 191.

Astronauts use diapers during take-off and landing and while on spacewalks.

### 192.

Astronauts avoid eating beans as a single episode of flatulence in space could rip a space suit apart.

### 193.

In the 19th century, scientists observed the fast evolution of the peppered moth's colour near Manchester, UK. Caused by the air pollution, it has been dubbed "one of the clearest and most easily understood examples of Darwinian evolution in action".

### 194.

Two out of every three US citizens do not have a passport.

### 195.

At Kuala Lumpur's airport, Malaysia, someone abandoned three Boeing 747s on the tarmac and never took them back. In late 2015, the airport placed an ad in the local newspapers asking for help in identifying their owner.

### 196.
Van Halen, Whitesnake, Motley Crew, U2 and other rock bands have been sued by fans for hearing damage during a concert.

### 197.
In 1943, Project Habakkuk was discussed in detail by the UK military. In short, they planned to construct an aircraft carrier out of *pykrete* (a mixture of wood pulp and ice, named after Geoffrey Pyke) for use against Nazi U-boats in the mid-Atlantic.

### 198.
Cambodia, Malaysia and Vatican City are the only existent elective monarchies.

### 199.
Cat's eyes (the retroreflective road safety devices) were invented in 1934.

200.
There are freshwater sharks in Lake Nicaragua, Nicaragua.

201.
Myspace refused to buy Facebook on two occasions.

202.
Lobsters can grow new eyeballs.

203.
Eyebrows have on average 550 hairs.

204.
On average, we blink four million times every year.

205.
In a lifetime, a human would spend three years on the toilet.

206.
Hair loss increases in autumn.

207.
Astronauts lose their sense of smell in space.

208.
Bangladesh used to be called East Pakistan until 1971.

209.
Grinding your teeth is a condition known as *bruxism*.

210.
In Liechtenstein, the gender ratio at birth is 126 males for every 100 females (data as of 2016).

211.
Airplane tickets are statistically the most expensive to buy on a Saturday.

212.
There are no ants in Iceland, Greenland and Antarctica.

213.
A Canadian company sells canned air to China.

214.
Uruguay produces almost 100% of its electricity out of renewable sources.

215.
75% of children eat the ears of chocolate bunnies first.

216.

Finland has the world's highest coffee consumption
per capita – 12 kg (25 pounds) each year.

217.

Women are more likely to cheat on their partner in
the weeks before and after their birthday than in any
other period of the year.

218.

In the English language, no sovereign state in the
world (member of the UN) has a name starting with
the letters W and X.

219.

There are many "volcanoes" on Triton (Neptune's
largest moon). Instead of lava, they erupt ice!

220.

People in Iceland suffer twice less often from seasonal
affective disorder compared to the other Northern
countries at the same latitude and nobody
knows why.

221.

The IBM ThinkPad was the first laptop with a DVD-
ROM reader.

222.

Mickey Mouse was the first non-human to win an Oscar.

223.

The shootout scene of the movie "Heat" is shown to US Marine recruits as an example of how to retreat under enemy fire.

224.

The Mediterranean island of Mallorca (Spain) has the oldest tourist service worldwide, established more than 110 years ago.

225.

So far, only two Popes have visited Sweden.

226.

South Korea grants exemption from military service, which is mandatory for all able-bodied males countrywide, to all sportsmen who win a gold Olympic medal.

227.

In 2016, endohedral fullerene was the most expensive material worldwide. The price was set at USD 145 million per gram. It is used in GPS devices and atomic clocks for highly increased accuracy and precision.

228.

Retailers did the math – a more lenient return policy normally correlates with an increase in returns but also with a much greater surge in purchases.

229.

In 1848, Bern and Zurich were both striving to become the capital of Switzerland. In Bern, as a brave publicity move, they literally made wine flow from the city's fountains.

230.

Since 2016, one in three landline phone calls in the USA is made by robots.

231.

Samsung provides free smartphones for a period of up to five days to every foreign tourist visiting South Korea.

232.

Norway planned to give Finland a mountain peak as a gift for the latter's 100th birthday (on 6 December 2017). The peak would have become Finland's highest point. Administrative and legal difficulties however blocked the noble initiative.

233.

Deep Purple, the rock band, were inspired to write their hit "Smoke on the Water" by the fire that burnt down the Montreux Casino (Switzerland) in 1971.

234.

The Latvian soldier, Janis Pinups, deserted from the Red Army in 1944. He came out of hiding only in 1995, at the age of seventy, and turned himself in to the local police station.

235.

The last Japanese combatant from WWII, Lt. Hiroo Onada, only surrendered in 1974. He had been hiding in the jungle for twenty-nine years and was unaware that Japan had capitulated.

236.

Japan and Russia did not sign a peace treaty after WWII, meaning that in theory a state of war still exists between them.

237.

Andorra welcomes almost 2.5 million tourists every year. The small country holds the world record with thirty-three visitors per resident.

238.

The female hyena has a pseudo-penis, which is larger than the penis of the male hyena. A pseudo-penis is an animal body structure that, while superficially appearing to be a penis, is derived from a different developmental path.

239.

The hagfish is the only living animal to have a skull but no vertebral column.

240.

The airport in Stuttgart, Germany, was named after the local politician, Manfred Rommel. A little-known fact is that his father was Field Marshal Erwin Rommel (aka the Desert Fox): one of the most successful German commanders during World War II.

241.

Australia has not experienced a recession for the last twenty-five years.

242.

Up until the early 19th century, the conductor of a musical orchestra would also play an instrument during the performance.

243.

Asphalt was first used as a road building material in Babylon, around 620 BCE, during the reign of King Nabopolassar.

244.

Jupiter and Saturn radiate more energy than they absorb from the Sun.

245.

Tom Cruise was the first actor to have five back-to-back hits that grossed more than 100 million dollars each in box office earnings.

246.

In Japan, 10 October 2006 was declared "Tom Cruise Day". Tom Cruise has made more trips to Japan than any other Hollywood star and was thus awarded his own day.

247.

Barra Airport, Scotland, is the only airport in the world where scheduled flights use a beach as a runway.

### 248.

Built by the Nazis between 1936 and 1939, the German beach resort named Prora has 10,000 rooms with sea view. However, it has never had a single guest.

### 249.

Saudi Arabia only switched to the "Western" Gregorian calendar in October 2016. Civil servants lost eleven days of salary as a result of this reform.

### 250.

In Lichtenstein, prison inmates with sentences over two years are normally confined abroad. They are sent to do their time in Austrian prisons.

### 251.

The foods your mother ate while pregnant with you are likely to influence what your favourite foods will be.

### 252.

In 2012, a Belgian man filed for divorce after nineteen years of marriage after finding out that his wife had been born a man.

### 253.

There are registered cases of dying of laughter.

### 254.

The engine oil of Aston Martin Vulcan can be changed in less than 100 seconds. For most other car models, the usual time is fifteen minutes.

### 255.

In parts of Germany, it is illegal to wash your car on Sunday. It is also illegal to run out of fuel on highways.

### 256.

Bullfighting is not an ancient tradition at all. It started in the 18th century in Andalusia, Spain.

### 257.

Empty batteries bounce when dropped, charged ones do not.

**258.**

The spacecraft Voyager was initially named
Mariner Jupiter/Saturn.

**259.**

Jupiter's moon Io is so volcanically active that its
surface is no more than 1,000 years old.

**260.**

Sri Lanka was known by the name of Ceylon
until 1948.

**261.**

A UK filmmaker shot a movie that shows just a freshly
painted wall drying for fourteen hours. Why? He had a
gripe with the British Film Board, all of whom are
obliged by law to watch all films that are to be
screened in the United Kingdom.

**262.**

Figs are one of the oldest fruits grown by humans.

**263.**

In 2009, the Brazilian environment group SOS Mata
Atlantica urged people to pee in the shower in a bid to
conserve water.

264.

The tiny country of Luxembourg is the largest
investment fund centre in Europe and
the second largest in the world after the USA.

265.

Up to 10% of all paper towels in the gym are used to
wipe the water off one's shower gel bottle.

266.

A UK Paralympic swimmer was disqualified from the
IPC European Championships S8 100m freestyle final
for failing to cover up his Olympic rings tattoo in
May 2016.

267.

Pyotr Tchaikovsky's ballet Swan Lake was inspired by
the real life story of the Bavarian King Ludwig II.

268.

There is more information about the Virgin Mary in
the Quran than in the Bible.

269.

Male mosquitos have large, feather-like antennas and
can be visually distinguished from females.

270.

Theoretically, a female mosquito can produce about 150 million eggs in a single year.

271.

Sweaty people and pregnant women have a greater chance of being bitten by a mosquito.

272.

Hyperloop, Elon Musk's project for a levitating train with a theoretical top speed of over 1200 km/h (760 mph), started tests in early 2016. The prototype reached a top speed of 324 km/h (201 mph) in 2017, still far away from the ambitious goal.

273.

Multiple studies show that men are more likely to marry and stay married to women who bear them sons rather than daughters.

274.

Pistachios can combust spontaneously.

275.

The B52 bomber entered in service in 1955 and is expected to be used by the United States Air Force until 2040.

276.

China's "one family-one child" policy lasted from 1979 to 2015.

277.

Pope Benedict IX was elected pope at the tender age of eleven.

278.

The Palace of the Parliament in Romania is the heaviest and the second largest (after the US Pentagon) building in the world.

279.
Elephants give birth after about two years
of pregnancy.

280.
Italy only legalised divorce in 1970.

281.
The Philippines remains the only UN-member state
without legal provision for divorce.

282.
There are no reptiles in Antarctica.

283.
The word "bistro" comes from Russian, where it
means "quick".

284.
Finland became the first country in the world to
launch its own emojis in 2015.

285.
Worldwide, 1.8 million Ikea meatballs are sold
every day.

### 286.
Orthodox Christians observe on average 200 days of fasting each year.

### 287.
To date (early 2018), the most bananas peeled and eaten in one minute by one person is eight. The record was set in 2012.

### 288.
The company Goodyear is now known for producing tyres. Decades ago, it was also a renowned producer of pillows.

### 289.
The largest rodent to ever exist was *Josephoartigasia Monesi*. It weighed up to one ton.

### 290.
In Italy, the number 17 is considered unlucky.

### 291.
Bangkok has many more residents than all the other thirty-one cities in Thailand combined.

### 292.
Nobody climbed Everest in 2015.

293.
Deaf Americans will be better understood in France than in the United Kingdom. US Sign Language was created by a Frenchman and it closely resembles the French Sign Language whereas UK Sign Language differs greatly.

294.
Norway is building the world's first underwater floating tunnel.

295.
The construction of a 3-km pipeline from a brewery to the bottling plant in Bruges, Belgium, was crowdfunded. The contributors will receive a bottle of beer every day for the rest of their lives.

296.
A study found out that people who use their integrated browser (Internet Explorer or Safari) have a greater chance to do badly in their job and to be fired than those who use an additionally installed one (such as Firefox or Chrome).

297.
Lew Wallace wrote "Ben Hur". Did you know that he also served as a governor of the US state of New Mexico and promised to pardon Billy the Kid?

298.
Each year, more than 80 million tourists visit France. Their number exceeds that of the entire population of the country.

299.
The city of Shanghai hosts the first Disneyland in China.

300.
The US state with the most numerous plane flyovers is Virginia.

301.
The Ford Pinto car was not a success in Brazil as "pinto" is slang for "small penis".

302.
On any given day, women lose almost twice as many hairs as men.

303.
During WWII, the US Army used code-talkers to transmit encoded messages in the Navajo Indian language, as this made them indecipherable to Japanese intelligence.

304.

Right after WWI, Germany made bicycles "tyres" out of metal springs due to rubber shortages.

305.

The encircled "U" sign on food labels means it is kosher.

306.

The Soviet pilot, Ivan Chisov, survived a fall from an altitude of 7 km (23,000 ft) with no parachute in 1942. He was able to fly again just three months later.

307.

The drink Fanta originated in Nazi Germany during WWII. Local soda drink factories could no longer import the original Coca-Cola syrup from the USA due to the trade embargo and had to improvise with available ingredients, leading to the genesis of the world's favourite orange soda.

### 308.
The Dutch police use eagles to catch drones flying illegally in airport areas.

### 309.
A flatworm called planarian can fully regenerate from a 1/279 piece of its body over the course of several weeks.

### 310.
The founder of the automotive company Honda, Soichiro Honda, decided to choose his successor amongst his employees, neglecting his family members – quite a rebellious move against the Japanese traditions at the time.

### 311.
Switzerland has four official languages. As a compromise, none of them is used on the country's postal stamps. Instead Latin is used.

### 312.
In 2016, Granit and Taulant Xhaka became the first brothers to ever play against each other at the European Championship football finals. They represented Switzerland and Albania respectively.

### 313.

Three-quarters of the Swiss voters rejected UN membership in a referendum in 1986. Switzerland held another one in 2002 and eventually joined the United Nations.

### 314.

In many cases, toddlers recognise companies' logos before they are able to recognise their own name.

### 315.

The blue whale cannot swallow anything bigger than a grapefruit.

### 316.

Charles Dickens coined the word "boredom".

### 317.

Luxembourg is planning to mine asteroids. Many asteroids are known to contain minerals, metals and volatile gases invaluable to human life.

### 318.

Soldiers in the German Military Forces are allowed to disobey any order that, according to their conscience, they think would violate human dignity.

319.

Two out of every three US soldiers who served in
Vietnam were volunteers.

320.

The vast majority of children under the age of six
dream about animals.

321.

45% of Russia is covered with forests. These forests
roughly equal the total area of the continent Australia.

322.

35,000 Americans buy an insurance covering the risk
of "abduction by aliens" every year.

323.

The Russky Bridge in Vladivostok, Russia, is the
world's longest cable-stayed bridge. Built in 2012, it
cost over one billion US dollars, but is now virtually
unused. It has a capacity of 50,000 cars per day while
the existing population of Russky Island is
5,000 people.

324.

Esther de Figueiredo Ferraz became the first female
minister in Brazil in 1982.

325.

The ozone actually smells like geranium.

326.

Elvis Presley's first TV appearance was on
9 September 1956.

327.

The Goliath Frog – the largest one on Earth – is mute.

328.

A Cherokee Indian, Sequoyah, aka George Guess,
invented their written alphabet – the only known case
when an illiterate invented a written language.

### 329.

The Cherokee Native Americans refer to themselves as *Ani-Yunwiya* (meaning "Principal People") and not as "Cherokee". In their language, the sounds "ch" and "r" simply do not exist.

### 330.

Jimi Hendrix, Dolly Parton and Cher claimed to be of Cherokee descent.

### 331.

Initially, there was no hole in the baskets used to play basketball. The hole appeared only twenty-one years after the invention of the sport.

### 332.

An axon (the part of a nerve cell which transmits impulses to other cells) in the giraffe's body can be up to 5 m (18 ft) long.

### 333.

Dolphins are the mammals with the most teeth. The long-snouted spinner dolphin has up to 252 teeth.

### 334.

The sound of a "shrimp layer" is the only natural noise that can totally jam a submarine's sonar, deafening its operators.

335.

Owned by the German company Daimler AG, the brand Mercedes-Benz first appeared in 1926. Until then, Daimler only produced typewriters and bicycles.

336.

The capital of Egypt, Cairo, was named after the planet Mars.

337.

Camel racing jockeys in the United Arab Emirates are being gradually replaced by robots since 2005.

338.

The Roman emperor, Nero Claudius Caesar, frequently sent runners into the mountains for snow, which he then flavoured with fruits and juices, thus almost inventing ice cream.

### 339.

All high school graduates from Kalamazoo, Michigan (USA) can attend any in-state college for free, thanks to a group of anonymous donors.

### 340.

Patients in several US states already have access to telemedicine, which allows consultative, diagnostic and treatment services via live video.

### 341.

Queens, New York (USA) has a ratio of 1:1 of native-born to foreign-born residents.

### 342.

In 1985, Tipper and Al Gore instigated a US Senate hearing, aiming to introduce a system that would label music albums for offensive material. The Gores questioned the morals of Twisted Sister's frontman, Dee Snider, while he testified. Ironically, the Gores recently divorced while Dee still has a solid marriage and family.

### 343.

The North Dakota Legislative Assembly (USA) has no permanent staff. Even the governor drives himself around! The State Assembly works four months out of every two years.

344.

Diamond is not the hardest substance on Earth.
In 2009, scientists announced that lonsdaleite (aka
hexagonal diamond) and wurtzite boron nitride both
have greater indentation strengths.

345.

Less than 25% of all snake species are venomous.

346.

On 24 August 2007, some 50 km (over 30 mi) of the
Pacific shoreline in Australia was covered with thick
foam. The media called this phenomenon
"Cappuccino Coast".

347.

In 2017, it cost on average 219 dollars for a US family of four to attend a Major League Baseball game.

348.

In New York, USA, it was illegal for men to show a nipple in public until 1936.

349.

Grab a calculator: dividing 1 by 998,001 gives you a really weird result.

350.

The indigenous peoples of Greenland use the Danish language (and not their native language Kalaallisut) if they need to count to more than twelve.

351.

There are still isolated tribes in the Andaman archipelago (between India and Malaysia) that cannot make fire.

352.

In South Korea and Japan, writing a person's name in red ink traditionally means that the person is deceased.

353.

Berlin, Germany, has around 1,700 bridges, several times more than Venice, Italy.

354.

In 2010, Bhutan banned tobacco sales and distribution.

355.

The Briton, Captain Robert Campbell, was captured by the Germans in August 1914. He was the only WWI prisoner-of-war who was given short leave to see his dying mother in the UK. The officer kept his promise and returned to the camp afterwards.

356.

One third of the inhabitants of Kaiserslautern, Germany, are American citizens. The city hosts one of the largest communities of US military personnel outside of the USA.

357.

Play-Doh (a modelling compound used by young children for art and craft projects) was initially used as a wallpaper cleaner. It was first manufactured in Cincinnati, Ohio (USA) in the 1930s.

358.

Many Olympic swimmers wear a swim cap under their swim cap. Two caps are thought to have a slight performance-enhancing effect and to better secure a swimmer's goggles.

359.

The national football team of Iceland made it to the quarter-final stage of Euro 2016. It is estimated that 9% of the entire population of the country were physically present at the stadium.

360.

The partridge often sleeps lying on the ground with its legs in the air.

361.

A Hijab can now form part of an official police uniform in Scotland and Canada.

362.

The famous German politician, Konrad Adenauer, invented the soy sausage during WWI. He could not patent it in Germany, but received a British patent after the war.

363.

All the numbers on a roulette table add up to 666.

364.

The US flag's official colours are called "Old Glory Red", "White", and "Old Glory Blue".

365.

Graça Machel is the only woman so far to have been the first lady of two separate countries. She was the First Lady of Mozambique from 1975 to 1986 and the First Lady of South Africa from 1998 to 1999.

366.

Easter is the peak time for reading crime stories and detective novels in Norway.

367.

Between 1958 and 1961, the United Arab Republic was a state and a short-lived political union between Egypt and Syria. It was dissolved in 1961, when Syria seceded.

368.

There are documented cases when dental floss facilitated prison escapes. It was either used to meticulously cut bars or braided together into a rope.

369.

In Moscow, Russia, you can receive your subway ticket free of charge in exchange of some physical exercise. All you have to do is to perform thirty squats in front of the ticketing machine.

370.

The Bazaar of Tabriz, Iran, is the largest covered market in the world. Founded in the 12th century, the complex covers an area of 0.3 km² (0.1 sq mi), and is only a bit smaller than the world's tiniest country, Vatican City.

371.

After 52 years of domination in its home car market,
Volvo lost the title of best-selling brand in Sweden
in 2016. Volkswagen simply outsold it.

372.

At the outbreak of World War II, one of the highest-
ranking officers in the British Army was the Japanese
emperor Hirohito! He held the honorary rank of
field marshal.

373.

In late 2016, the Bank of England confirmed that the
new £5 notes would contain animal fat. In response,
many vegans organised protests.

374.

One can become an air traffic controller in the United
States of America without a bachelor's degree.

375.

The US Army introduced multiple choice tests
during WWI.

376.

Worldwide, nine out of every ten people who learn
Finnish as a foreign language were motivated by their
interest in Finnish heavy metal music.

377.

Bob Dylan won a Nobel Prize for Literature in 2016. He became the first songwriter to ever win the prestigious award.

378.

After the dissolution of the USSR, many Russians could not prove their working experience when applying for a pension. Several former communist leaders went so far as to present as a proof articles dedicated to them in newspapers and in the Encyclopaedia Britannica.

379.

A tiger's tongue is covered with many sharp rear-facing projections called *papillae*. They are designed to strip the skin, feathers, fur and meat right off prey.

380.

The only indigenous primates that live in Canada are humans.

381.

Normally, dolphins do not drink seawater. Like many sea mammals, they only obtain fresh water from their food.

382.

The state flag of Alaska (USA) was invented by a 13-year-old child.

383.

Lausanne, Switzerland, is the smallest city in the world to have a metro.

384.

Women's feet are two to three degrees Celsius colder than men's.

385.

*Pseudis paradoxa*, aka the paradoxical frog or shrinking frog, as a tadpole measures up to 25 cm (10 in). In the process of becoming an adult frog, it shrinks in size by three to four times.

386.

The distance covered by individual players in a football game was first tracked with technology "borrowed" from military fighter jets (namely the system used to lock onto and keep track of an enemy aircraft).

387.

Playing hockey is very popular in Canada. It is even depicted on the $5 banknote.

388.

When observed from an airplane, rainbows sometimes look like a discus and not like an arch.

389.

The house with the narrowest facade of Amsterdam, The Netherlands, is only 202 cm (less than 80 in) wide. The shape of the houses in Amsterdam is due to the tax rate in the Golden Age, which was calculated based on the width of the house.

390.

In 2013, Tesla Model S underwent crash evaluations. Habitually, cars are ranked on a scale of one to five stars. The Model S passed the tests so well that, if such a rating existed, it would have earned 5.4.

391.

To produce 1 ton of paper from standing timber you need more energy than to produce 1 ton of steel from iron.

392.

The Philippine tarsier is the mammal with the biggest eyes as a proportion to its body size.

393.

Madagascar hosts the world's only pirate graveyard.

394.

Several bird species are known to sleep while flying: swifts, albatrosses and great frigate birds to name a few.

395.

The former Cuban leader, Fidel Castro, appeared in two Hollywood movies in his youth.

396.

The pioneer of television, Philo Farnsworth, got inspired when observing rows of vegetables in a field.

397.

A large part of the Netherlands is actually below the sea level, with the lowest city (Nieuwekerk aan den IJssel) at -7 m (-23 ft).

398.

The game of Scrabble was banned in Romania in the 1980s. The Romanian President, Nicolae Ceausescu, perceived it as "overly intellectual" and a "subversive evil".

399.

There are no woodpeckers in Australia, New Guinea, New Zealand and Madagascar.

400.

The Australian Aboriginals never developed bows and arrows.

401.

The famous artist, Salvador Dali, designed the logo of Chupa Chups lollipops.

402.

Until 2010, beekeeping was illegal in New York City, USA.

403.

Venezuela's name roughly translates as "the little Venice".

404.

Some animals, such as alligators and platypuses, use their tails to store fat.

405.

Initially, the WD-40 spray was developed for lubricating nuclear missiles.

406.

"Hitler woman" is an anagram of "mother-in-law".

407.

The British royal family are not allowed to play Monopoly at home.

### 408.

Portugal, Spain, Ireland, Finland and all the former USSR states have different rails sizes from the rest of Europe. This specificity means that trains from these countries cannot travel in Europe without changes to the wheelsets.

### 409.

If we were capable of hearing frequencies lower than 20 Hz, we would hear the movement of our muscles.

### 410.

The Japanese macaques, aka "snow monkeys", are the most northern-living primates. They are sometimes observed rolling snowballs for fun.

## 411.

In 2005, the company 3M set up a promotional stunt at a bus stop in Vancouver, Canada. They left cash behind their unbreakable glass and encouraged passers-by to try to break it and get the promised three million dollars. No-one succeeded.

## 412.

Every year, more than 70,000 whales die in the oceans from natural causes.

## 413.

Volvo, Mercedes and Google announced in 2015 that they would accept all liability when their cars are driven in autonomous mode.

## 414.

The percent sign % was first used around 1650 CE.

## 415.

Elderly people dream in black and white more often than youths. One of the possible explanations is that they grew up in an era of black-and-white television.

## 416.

The city of Dubai, UAE, began testing driverless flying cars to be used as a drone taxi service in late 2017.

### 417.

Quebec, the French speaking Canadian province, produces two thirds of the world's pure maple syrup.

### 418.

The Ferrari F40 became the first production car to break the 320 km/h (200 mph) threshold in 1987.

### 419.

As of today, the Gotthard Base Tunnel is the longest railway tunnel in the world. It goes through the Swiss Alps and boasts a route length of 57 km (35.5 mi).

### 420.

A cricket's ears are located on its front legs, just below the knees.

### 421.

Up to 90% of animals in the ocean depths are bioluminescent.

422.

In Italy, they refer to the colour of the egg yolks as "red".

423.

In 1983, an Israeli Air Force F15 jet fighter lost one wing but nevertheless successfully landed in the Negev desert, Israel.

424.

The Hanover Fairground (Germany) is the largest exhibition ground in the world. It boasts almost 500,000 m² (5.3 million sq ft) of covered indoor space.

### 425.

In early 2016, Sir Paul McCartney (a former Beatles member) was refused entry to a party, as the party was "VIP only". He commented: "How VIP do I gotta get?"

### 426.

Many plants can chemically "feel" who is eating their leaves (caterpillars or deer) and counteract by releasing tailor-made defensive chemicals.

### 427.

When full, Hoover Dam is the largest reservoir in the United States of America by volume. By the way, it was initially called Boulder Dam.

428.

Absinthe (a highly alcoholic beverage) was illegal to import or manufacture in many European countries in the period 1910 to 2000.

429.

Mount Everest has 4G mobile phone coverage since 2013.

430.

Some companies offer the rental of high quality baby clothes. It is cheaper than buying and environmentally friendly, as those clothes can last up to eleven cycles.

431.

Taller and older women give birth to twins more often.

432.

If the temperature is too low, snakes cannot digest food.

433.

Some desert snails can survive more than five years without water and food, at temperatures of up to 50 °C (122 °F).

434.

46 BCE was the longest year with its 445 days. Julius Caesar added two extra leap months as a preparation for his calendar reform, which he implemented in 45 BCE.

435.

The Yamoussoukro Basilica, formally Basilique Notre-Dame de la Paix, is a Roman Catholic church in Yamoussoukro, Cote d'Ivoire. It is the largest Christian church building in the world.

### 436.

Jonas Salk invented the killed-virus polio vaccine in the early 1950s and first tested it on himself and his family. He deliberately did not patent the vaccine.

### 437.

Painted swamp turtles can not only freeze and then thaw, but also hold their breath for months as the water above them freezes.

### 438.

A tick larva can live more than one year without food (i.e. blood).

### 439.

The Scandinavian snus is a form of smokeless tobacco which is usually placed under the upper lip and does not provoke spitting. Its sale is illegal in the European Union except for Sweden.

### 440.

In 2014, a study found a direct link between the frequency of selfies and the tendency toward psychopathy and narcissism.

### 441.

All adult amphibious animals are carnivores.

442.

The film actor, director and producer, Jackie Chan, is also a trained opera singer.

443.

"Desire path" or "desire line" is a shortcut created by human traffic outside paved alleys.

444.

Adult mayflies live only a few hours. They do not sleep at all until they die.

445.

Romans did not have an equivalent word for "interesting".

446.

Whales have eardrums larger in diameter than their throats.

447.

Measured from the centre of Earth, Rio de Janeiro, Brazil, is higher than the Himalayas.

448.

Francium was discovered in 1939. It was the last chemical element to be found in nature.

449.

Batman is a town in south-eastern Turkey.

450.

Only flamingos, pigeons and some penguins produce "milk". Crop milk is a secretion from the lining of the crop of parent birds that is regurgitated to young birds.

451.

Denmark is by far the world leader in the incineration of household waste, burning some 80% of the local waste.

452.

Metropolis, the home of Superman, really exists (in Illinois, USA).

453.

In 1940, fearing a Nazi invasion, Winston Churchill moved most of the British wealth (in gold and securities) to Canada. It was called Operation Fish.

454.

The Rio 2016 Paralympic Games (Brazil) were the first to introduce medals that Paralympic Athletes can hear.

### 455.

Iowa is the only US state whose name starts with two vowels.

### 456.

The speed camera was invented by a Dutch racing driver, Maus Gatsonides.

### 457.

In 2013, two wannabe robbers armed with squirt guns entered Clifton Grill restaurant in Chicago, USA. The owner asked them to return in an hour since he was busy. The two men actually came back only to be caught by the police.

### 458.

On several occasions, pigeons were arrested in India on suspicion of being spies.

### 459.

Sometimes, the automatic face-blurring technology used by Google Street View also blurs the faces of... cows.

### 460.

The inventor of the pacemaker, Wilson Greatbatch, also invented the lithium battery.

461.
Iceland switches off street lights so that everyone can enjoy the *aurora borealis* (the Northern Lights).

462.
With his invention, the Gatling gun, Richard Jordan Gatling actually hoped to stop the carnage of the American Civil War. He drew inspiration from a seed planting device he had patented in his youth.

463.
In 1943, the US Supreme Court ruled that forcing public schoolchildren to salute the flag violates the First Amendment.

464.

The President of Uganda (from 1971 to 1979) designed his own title: "His Excellency, President for Life, Field Marshal Al Hadji Doctor Idi Amin Dada... Lord of All the Beasts of the Earth and Fishes of the Seas and Conqueror of the British Empire in Africa in General and Uganda in Particular". He also claimed to be the official uncrowned King of Scotland.

465.

Ramesses II was the most powerful pharaoh of Ancient Egypt. In 1974, his mummy started rapidly deteriorating and was sent for scientific examinations to Paris, France. He was issued an Egyptian passport on which his occupation was listed as "King (deceased)". He was received at the airport with full military honours, on a red carpet, like any other visiting head of state.

466.

The first cash machine (ATM) was installed on 27 June 1967 by Barclays Bank in its Enfield Town branch in London, United Kingdom.

467.

In 2016, the University of California, USA, published a study which says in short that if you have increasing difficulties to detect sarcasm, you might be developing dementia.

468.

Many aircraft engines are designed to be cooled by the fuel.

469.

In 1964, the Soviet spy, Igor Ivanov, became the only person to be released on bail after a US Federal Court jury had sentenced him to 30 years for espionage. He never went to prison.

470.

In early 2015, Dr Michal Kosinski created a computer model that could predict someone's personality better than their spouse could. The model only needs the background knowledge of this person's 150 Facebook likes.

471.

The actor, John Cazale, appeared in five movies. They were all nominated for the Oscar Academy Award for Best Picture.

472.

Young rhinos can regrow a horn.

473.

Many keyboards have proved to be more efficient than QWERTY (patented back in 1868). However, we are so used to it that QWERTY remains by far the most popular keyboard.

474.

Krishna is the name of one of the Hindu gods. According to the legends, he had more than 16,000 wives.

### 475.

In 1849, Henry Brown, a Virginia slave, successfully shipped himself to freedom. He travelled almost 600 km (370 mi) in a custom-made box (parcel) to Philadelphia, USA.

### 476.

Monaco and Indonesia have virtually the same national flag. The only slight difference is the size ratio.

### 477.

In March 2017, the Chinese government closed down the last coal power plant in the Beijing area. They switched to natural gas instead in a bid to fight the heavy smog over the Chinese capital.

### 478.

In 2006, Honda introduced the first airbag for motorbikes.

### 479.

The actors who voiced Mickey and Minnie Mouse were married.

### 480.

In the period 1998-2016, none of the sumo champions was born in Japan.

481.

Papua-New Guinea has a population of seven million people and roughly the size of Sweden. They speak an estimated 850 languages (of all 6000 known worldwide), belonging to dozens of distinct language families.

482.

*Alvinella pompejana*, the Pompeii worm, is a species of deep-sea worm that can survive in temperatures as high as 80 °C (176 °F).

483.

Darts rules prohibit drinking alcohol during the game.

484.

On average, it takes cork oaks forty years before they can produce good cork.

485.

The residents of the District of Columbia (United States of America) voted for the first time for US President on 3 November 1964.

486.

The city of Cincinnati in Ohio, USA, was named after the Roman general Cincinnatus.

### 487.

Mikheil Saakashvili was a politician in two countries. Initially, he was President of Georgia. Then he was granted Ukrainian citizenship (losing his Georgian one) and became Governor of Odessa, Ukraine. Since July 2017, he is stateless as he was stripped of his Ukrainian citizenship.

### 488.

The Hotel Moskva in Moscow, Russia, was notable for the use of two different designs for the façade. Allegedly, the architect submitted to Stalin a single drawing where each half showed a different design. Stalin put his signature exactly in the middle and as no-one dared to ask for clarification, they simply built an asymmetric hotel.

### 489.

Over 4,000 islands in Indonesia are still unmanaged and without names. In January 2017, the Indonesian government announced that if foreign investors develop an island, they could name it as they wish.

### 490.

Pepsi was initially called "Brad's Drink". In 1893, it was introduced by Caleb Bradham in New Bern, North Carolina (USA).

491.

Unlike most mammals, humans, primates, guinea pigs and bats have lost their ability to produce vitamin C.

492.

Worldwide, more IKEA catalogues are printed than Bibles.

493.

Every two-dimensional map of Earth is distorted.

494.

DVD players, computers and toasters were banned in Cuba until 2008.

495.

The middle name of the Hollywood actor, Richard Gere, is Tiffany.

496.

The famous singer, Elvis Presley, was a natural blond.

497.

Among all animals, the crocodiles have the highest concentration of acid in their stomach.

498.

Ouija boards were initially made of coffin wood. The first Ouija patent was awarded without any explanation on how the device worked.

499.

Nile crocodiles have a brain that continues growing all their life.

500.

General Electric is the only still operating independent company that was part of the original Dow Jones indcx of 1896.

501.

Istanbul, Turkey, is the largest city that occupies two continents.

502.

Turkey has only 3% of its territory in Europe. The country applied for membership in the European Union in 1987 and is still awaiting accession.

503.

On average, in Kericho, Kenya, there is hail falling one out of every three days.

504.
The African country of Morocco applied for membership in the European Union in 1987. The application was rejected.

505.
Owls cannot move or roll their eyes.

506.
According to the Chinese law on the "Management Measures for the Reincarnation of Living Buddhas in Tibetan Buddhism" from 2007, Buddhist monks need to seek prior government approval before reincarnation.

507.
Around 1780, the so-called Industrial Revolution started in the United Kingdom, making it the first industrialised country worldwide. Since 2016 however, the UK has been making more money from rock 'n' roll than from coal and steel.

508.
In 2013, a white US supremacist and racist, Craig Cobb, agreed to undergo a genetic test and receive the results on live television. He turned out to be genetically 14% Sub-Saharan African.

509.
In 19th-century Scotland, *"shit-faced"* used to mean "to have a childish face".

510.
*"Ascorbic"* means "anti-scurvy". Ascorbic acid in fact effectively prevents the disease.

511.
Some fourteen years before the sinking of Titanic, the novel called "Futility, or the Wreck of the Titan" by Morgan Robertson had described a ship called Titan, travelling on the same route at almost the same speed, sinking after a collision with an iceberg.

## 512.

In 1913, Adolf Hitler, Joseph Stalin, Leon Trotsky (the founding leader of the Soviet Red Army), Josip Broz Tito (President for Life of Yugoslavia) and Sigmund Freud (the founder of psychoanalysis) all lived within a few kilometres of each other in Vienna, then Austro-Hungarian Empire.

## 513.

Silk thrown at a brick wall would stick to the wall; cheaper artificial fabrics would normally slide down.

## 514.

Elks have two ivory teeth, which are believed to be the remnants of the tusks from their ancestors.

## 515.

The Battle of Sedan was fought during the Franco-Prussian War from 1 to 2 September 1870. To commemorate this major German victory, which by the way made the unification of Germany possible, 2 September was celebrated as an unofficial national holiday in Germany until 1919.

## 516.

Nowadays, only Cyprus and Kosovo have a map on their national flag.

517.

During WWII, the paper clip was a symbol of the Norwegian resistance.

518.

Maybe you have noticed that the heads of LEGO figures have a hole. Its sole purpose is to prevent choking.

519.

LEGO originates from the Danish phrase "leg godt", which means "play good".

520.

LEGO recently created Anti-LEGO slippers. Anyone who has stepped barefoot on a LEGO block knows the pain...

### 521.

In May 2016, an Australian senator gave a speech to the Parliament while breastfeeding her child. The little girl became the first baby to be breastfed in the Australian Parliament.

### 522.

Spider-Man comics inspired the electronic bracelet.

### 523.

In Massachusetts, USA, tattooing was illegal up until 2000.

### 524.

In Mexico, Austria and Germany the law recognizes that it is basic human nature to escape for freedom and hence the act of prison escape itself is not a crime.

### 525.

DNA analyses proved that Polynesians introduced chickens to South America (Peru) well before Christopher Columbus reached the New World.

### 526.

The earliest documents containing written human names are approximately 5,500 years old.

527.

Aitabdel Salem spent nearly five months in a US jail —
from November 2014 to April 2015 — unaware of the
fact that his bail was only 2 dollars.

528.

Pearl Jam is a US rock band that released seventy-two
live albums in the period 2000 - 2001.

529.

The giant panda is the only bear that
does not hibernate.

530.

Warner Bros film studio has officially confirmed that
Tweety is a canary.

531.

Formosa is the old name of Taiwan. It was widely
used up until the early 20th century.

532.

The Allied forces deployed more troops for
the Battle of Okinawa (1945) than for the D-Day
in Normandy (1944).

### 533.

In Turkey, the Ulas family is better known as "The Family That Walks on All Fours". Debate still exists as to the nature and cause of their quadruped gait.

### 534.

In 1999, Bulgaria gave as a gift more than one hundred T-55 battle tanks and other pieces of weaponry to the neighbouring Former Yugoslav Republic of Macedonia. Several years later, FYROM proceeded to sell many of the tanks and cashed in the gift.

### 535.

In early 2017, a French businessman sued Uber for €45 million ($48 million) after his wife received notifications of his trips to his mistress and later filed for divorce.

### 536.

Across the cultures, women want a husband on average 3.5 years older than them, while men seek 2.5-year-younger wives.

### 537.

The Emperor of Japan is not allowed to eat fugu (pufferfish). This fish contains tetrodotoxin which can be lethally poisonous.

538.

Sean Connery's character James Bond was the first to say on screen "shaken, not stirred". Careful readers will notice that in every book, on average, James Bond has a drink every seven pages.

539.

Germany was the first country ever to implement Daylight Saving Time in order to save energy during World War I.

540.

Bootlace worms are one of the longest animals, with specimens up to 55 m (180 ft) long. In the same time, they are among the simplest organisms with a separate mouth and anus.

### 541.
Saint Patrick is the patron of Nigeria since 1961.

### 542.
The Huzhu Pagoda, China, and the Tower of Church of Suurhusen, Germany, are both more tilted than the famous Tower of Pisa, Italy.

### 543.
A US tea trader accidentally invented tea bags in 1904. Thomas Sullivan started packing samples of his tea into silk bags, which his clients mistakenly began to put directly into the hot water without unpacking.

### 544.
The Easter Bilby is the Australian alternative to the Easter Bunny.

545.

In 1987, a US court admitted for the first time DNA as evidence. The United Kingdom followed suit the year after.

546.

Elmo Monster (the Muppet character) was the first non-human to testify before the US Congress in 2002. He urged support for increased funding for music education.

547.

Cans of regular soda are denser than water and sink. Cans of diet soda are usually less dense than water and float.

548.

The German retailer, Otto, uses artificial intelligence (AI) to purchase goods. With no human intervention, AI is predicting with 90% accuracy what will be sold within thirty days and automatically buys more than 200,000 items every month from third-party brands.

549.

In early 1915, almost ten million pigs were slaughtered in Germany to free up grain and potatoes for human consumption.

### 550.
Up until 1946, in the Japanese schools they were teaching mythology instead of history.

### 551.
In Portugal, each canteen which receives public money is obliged by law to offer a non-meat option.

### 552.
In 2015, on average one billion dollars were given daily for charity in the United States of America.

### 553.
Dutch names can sound hilarious in English. How about Kitty Miao, Justin Case, or an eye doctor called I.C. Notting?

### 554.
In 1979, China invaded Vietnam because Vietnam had invaded Cambodia and had ousted the notorious Khmers Rouges, supported by China. The conflict lasted a month and the Chinese army withdrew from Vietnam. Both sides claimed a victory.

### 555.
Upon their return from the Moon in 1969, the US astronauts had to fill in a customs declaration.

556.
Bolivian capital La Paz has the world's largest aerial cable car urban transit system. It is called *Mi Teleférico* and as of early 2018 has a length of 17.3 km (10.7 mi).

557.
In 2016, the clothing brand H&M increased the age diversity of its swimsuit models by hiring a 60-year-old woman, Gillean McLeod.

558.
The origin of the word "dog" remains one of the greatest mysteries of English etymology.

### 559.
In 2005, a mock-paper titled "Get me off your fucking mailing list" has been accepted and published in the International Journal of Advanced Computer Technology.

### 560.
In 2016, Judge Lou Olivera from Fayetteville, North Carolina (USA), sentenced Sgt. Joseph Serna, a veteran with post-traumatic stress disorder, to 24 hours in jail. The compassionate judge (a veteran himself) then joined the prisoner behind bars and the two spent the night talking.

### 561.
The Ancient Romans had an eight-day week. They switched to the seven-day week in 321 CE.

### 562.
Ray-Ban sunglasses were the first ones to introduce an anti-glare filter.

### 563.
The largest shopping mall in the world, the New South China Mall (in Dongguan, China), covers an area twice as big as Vatican City, the world's smallest country.

### 564.

Nelson Rolihlahla Mandela became the first black head of state of South Africa in 1994. Before that, he had spent twenty-seven years in prison.

### 565.

Carlos Ghosn is the only CEO to have managed simultaneously two of the Fortune Global 500 companies.

### 566.

The vast majority of modern people have in their DNA between 1% and 4% of Neanderthal DNA.

### 567.

In 2010, Evan Muncie survived for twenty-seven days trapped in a huge pile of rubble after a massive earthquake struck Haiti.

### 568.

Stairwells in medieval castles were often curved very narrowly and in a clockwise direction. This design allowed the defenders to use their right hands in battle, thus handicapping the attackers.

### 569.

It is that simple: if a month starts with a Sunday, it will have a Friday the 13th.

570.
According to the rules of the International Tennis Federation, the tennis net can be up to 15 cm (6 in) lower in the middle.

571.
It was observed on many skyscrapers that the sun sets up to three minutes later on the top floor compared to the first floor.

572.
In the Star Wars saga, the sound of the TIE Fighter engines is actually a mix of an elephant call and a car driving on a wet pavement.

573.

The word "Jedi" is derived from Japanese word "jidaigeki", a genre of historical drama.

574.

In 1667, the Dutch swapped with Great Britain the island of Manhattan for Run Island, one of Indonesia's Banda Islands. Back then, the Indonesian islands were regarded as a precious source of spices.

575.

The word "vodka" derives from the Slavic word "voda", meaning "water".

576.

In 1698, the Russian emperor, Peter the Great, imposed a tax on beards in order to modernize the Russian society.

577.

A US company patented an automatic braking system capable of stopping the table saw within milliseconds after its blade comes in contact with the operator's hand. The inventor of SawStop, Steve Gass, used his own bare finger to demonstrate how safe his invention was.

578.
Mikhail Gorbachev was the first and only President of the USSR.

579.
The Russian President, Vladimir Putin, starred in a judo DVD.

580.
Russia covers 1/8 of the total land on Earth or 17 million km² (6.6 million sq mi). It is slightly more than the surface area of the dwarf-planet Pluto and roughly equal to the territories of the USA and Australia combined.

581.

In 1983, in what is known as "the Alraigo Incident", a lost UK Harrier fighter aircraft landed successfully on the deck of a Spanish container ship. The ship's crew and owners were awarded a compensation of £570,000 (USD 760,000).

582.

The Makonde tribe in Mozambique is a matrilineal society. Children and inheritances belong to women, and a husband moves into his wife's village.

# CHAPTER II

*Disturbing facts about our world*

## 1.

As of today, there are around 15,000 nuclear warheads worldwide, owned by the USA, Russia, France, China, the United Kingdom, Pakistan, India, Israel and North Korea.

## 2.

Airlines deal differently with in-flight deaths. Some major airlines keep body bags on-board just in case, while Singapore Airlines is known to have fitted the aircraft with special cupboards for corpses.

## 3.

Star Wars' character Anakin Skywalker (aka Darth Vader) meets six of the nine diagnostic criteria for Borderline Personality Disorder. Five are enough to make the diagnosis.

### 4.

In 2001, Turkmenistan outlawed opera, ballet, video games, listening to car radios, smoking in public and long hair on men.

### 5.

As of early 2016, the sixty-two richest people possessed more money than the rest of the world's population. According to another study from 2017, the eight world's richest people have the same wealth as the poorest 50% of the world population combined.

### 6.

5% of the entire population of North Korea serve in the army.

### 7.

In April 2016, North Korea proposed to halt its nuclear tests if the US stopped their annual military exercises with South Korea. The USA declined.

### 8.

In 2015, a Saudi millionaire was cleared of rape charges after telling a UK court that he accidentally penetrated an 18-year-old girl when he tripped and fell on her.

9.

Haiti experienced more hurricanes and earthquakes than any other country in the Western Hemisphere.

10.

A report from 2015 found traces of human DNA in hot dogs samples of several major US brands.

11.

In early 2016, a UK sexual offender was ordered to give the police 24 hours' notice before he has sex.

12.

During the first three months of World War II, more British died in car accidents in London due to the blackout rather than soldiers in battle.

13.

In early 2016, an Italian actor named Raphael Schumacher accidentally hanged himself to death during a theatre performance.

14.

In 1935, the Esperanto language was legally forbidden in Nazi Germany and many Esperantists ended up in concentration camps.

### 15.

Worldwide, deforestation claims an area roughly the size of Greece every year.

### 16.

Worldwide, Tonga has the highest rate of obesity.

### 17.

In 2003, the Moroccan government offered to the US troops in Iraq 2,000 monkeys, trained in detonating land mines.

### 18.

Bolivia was founded in 1825. On average, it has experienced one *coup d'état* per year of existence.

### 19.

The Louisiana Supreme Court (USA) ruled in October 2016 that Catholic priests are not obliged to report cases of sexual abuse of children if they learn about them during confession.

### 20.

Since 2014, US cops take more assets from people than burglars do. The US Civil Asset Forfeiture Act gives them the legal right to do so, even without filing charges.

### 21.
Tooth decay is the most common disease worldwide.

### 22.
In countries where abortions are outlawed, women are thirty-four times more likely to die of post-operative infections.

### 23.
Euthanasia Coaster is a hypothetic project of a machine in the form of a roller coaster, designed to take the life of a human being humanely.

### 24.
Romans used a sponge on the end of a stick instead of toilet paper.

### 25.

US women are twice as likely to die from pregnancy and childbirth complications as Canadian women.

### 26.

If there is a first class on a flight, passengers in the economy have 3.8 times greater chance to have an air rage fit, especially if they have to walk through first class to get to their seat.

### 27.

Over 50,000 Americans get injured in toilets each year.

### 28.

US President Ulysses S. Grant had a plan to buy the Dominican Republic for $1.6 million and to send there all four million freed black people.

### 29.

In medieval England, some wandering gipsies claimed to be descendants of the Egyptians and to be skilled fortune-tellers, thus deceiving and taking the money of many naïve locals. In 1530 CE, King Henry VIII decreed that impersonating an Egyptian was a serious crime and should be given the death sentence. By the way, the word "gipsy" derives from "Egyptian".

30.

In the late 1920s, General Motors secretly started purchasing trolley systems in many US cities. Its only aim was to dismantle them and turn them into bus lines.

31.

There are more prisoners in the USA than there are farmers.

32.

Walt Disney was an FBI informer.

33.

Monsanto produced the Agent Orange, a herbicide notorious for its use by the US forces in Vietnam.

34.

Tarantulas mothers kill 99% of their babies.

### 35.

In the USA, if you believe in a god you are twice as probable to end up in prison compared to non-believers. According to the 2014 General Sociological Survey, 21% of the Americans do not identify with a religion. At the same time, just 10.5% of US prison inmates are atheists.

### 36.

In Australia, bees kill more people than snakes do.

### 37.

Until 2002, the UK broadcaster BBC had banned the song "Gloomy Sunday" aka
"Hungarian Suicide song". It was thought to urge people to take their lives.

### 38.

Worldwide, the Republic of Guyana has the highest suicide rate.

### 39.

A five-star slum-like South African resort, Shanty Town, is supposed to give the rich tourists a taste of hard life. However, the shanties have running water, electricity, Wi-Fi, refrigerators, TV sets, and even floor heating.

40.

As of early 2018, China's CCTV surveillance network comprises about 200 million surveillance cameras and counting.

41.

In the late 1930s, the town of Yaphank, NY (USA) had streets named after Adolf Hitler and Joseph Goebbels.

42.

A 1% increase in unemployment in the USA leads to 40,000 premature deaths.

43.

The Ivanpah Solar Electric Generating System is a concentrated solar thermal plant in the Mojave Desert, USA. It generates up to 392 megawatts but burns about 6,000 birds every year.

44.

In 2015, a Disneyland employee, Darreck Enciso, attempted to trade Disneyland tickets for sex with an underage girl in the USA.

45.

During World War II, American servicemen used to take "trophies" from the corpses of Imperial Japanese troops.

46.

According to the World Health Organization, hairdressers have increased risk of developing cancer.

47.

In 2015, Martin Shkreli became the US most hated man for increasing the price of a life-saving medicine (for HIV-positive patients) from $13.50 to $750 per pill.

48.

Baltimore, Maryland, was the most dangerous city in the United States in 2017; Sunnyvale, California, the safest one.

49.

Tsetse flies kill about 70,000 people every year.

50.

During World War II, the Soviet Red Army executed 158,000 of its own soldiers; the German Wehrmacht: approximately 8,000.

51.

In Colorado, USA, losing an arm in a work-related accident would make the employer liable to pay no more than 36,000 dollars.

52.

Until 1997, cattle in the US were routinely fed with processed dead cats and dogs, which companies bought from shelters.

53.

US citizens who lived for more than six months in the UK in the period 1980-1996 are not allowed to donate blood. The reason is mad-cow disease prevention.

54.

If one eye of a baby monkey is covered with a bandage for the first two months after birth, this eye could stay blind forever.

### 55.

The only case when two democracies were at war occurred in 1941, with Great Britain declaring war on Finland.

### 56.

Nine out of ten black actresses nominated for an Oscar played characters who are or might soon become homeless.

### 57.

In 2002, the pop star Madonna was unhappy with air traffic noise above her English country estate and tried to buy the adjacent Dorset airport with the sole purpose to shut it down.

### 58.

Iowa, USA, wants to permit toddlers to use weapons. It could be a risky idea considering that in 2015 more US citizens were killed by toddlers with a gun than by terrorists.

### 59.

Even if both partners are HIV positive, they still need to use condoms during sex to prevent superinfection (i.e. being infected with a different strain of the virus). A superinfection increases the risk of acquiring drug resistance.

60.

Until as late as 1986, many doctors worldwide thought that babies could not feel pain. Therefore, many surgeries were performed on infants without anaesthesia.

61.

*Cymothoa exigua*, or the tongue-eating louse, is a parasite that eats a fish's tongue and takes its place.

62.

Upon his return to Colombia, the football player Andres Escobar was murdered for having scored an own goal which led to his national team's elimination from the 1994 FIFA World Cup.

## 63.

During World War II, a US pilot, Martin James Monti, defected to Nazi Germany with his airplane. Despite this, he was later allowed to reenlist in the US military.

## 64.

The Ides of March denarius is one of the few coins dedicated to a murder.

## 65.

One in nine black US children has had a parent in prison.

## 66.

It is more probable to catch a computer virus on a church website than on a porn website. The reason is that religious websites are often maintained by volunteers and not by IT professionals.

## 67.

Live pigeon shooting used to be an official Olympic sport.

## 68.

Only 30% of the global population have access to toilet paper.

69.

Less than 2% of what you spend on fries at the restaurant actually goes to the farmer who produced the potatoes.

70.

The famous Italian painter, Caravaggio, committed murder.

71.

In the US, the total number of prisoners increases by over 1,000 each week.

72.

On average, each year 12,000 miners die in accidents worldwide.

73.

In the Philippines, multiple karaoke bars have banned Frank Sinatra's song "My Way" as it is known to provoke riots and killings.

74.

Killed soldiers at Waterloo had their teeth extracted. Those very teeth were used as tooth "transplants" Europe-wide in the course of the next few decades.

## 75.

In Fiji, widows used to be strangled immediately after their husbands' death. When Fijians adopted Christianity, widow-strangling was abandoned.

## 76.

Since 2016, there have been several cases when starving Venezuelans broke into zoos and ate the exhibited animals.

## 77.

On average, seven people worldwide are diagnosed with heart cancer each year.

## 78.

Nicosia, Cyprus, is the only European capital that is still divided (walls, checkpoints, passport controls, etc.) into two parts.

## 79.

In October 2016, an atheist billboard in Nebraska, USA, reading "The Good Life Without God" had to be taken down following numerous complaints of pious citizens.

## 80.

Worldwide, icicles kill more people than sharks do.

81.

In the 1930s, the Nazi regime in Germany widely publicised a picture of the "Perfect Aryan Baby". Ironically, the baby chosen for the posters turned out to be Jewish.

82.

In 2014, Mubarak Bala, a Nigerian atheist, was forced to spend eighteen days in a psychiatric ward. It happened after his Muslim family declared him insane for not believing in their god.

## 83.

The then US President Bill Clinton forced Haiti to drop the import customs duties for rice in 1995. Soon afterwards Haiti was "flooded" with rice produced in Arkansas, USA.

## 84.

If intoxicated with methanol (contained in low quality alcohol drinks) you might be surprised to learn that the best antidote is ethanol (normal alcohol).

## 85.

Japanese women cannot remarry for six months after the divorce but men can.

## 86.

In 1975, a male participant in the famous bicycle race Tour de France gave a urine sample containing his wife's urine. He was found "pregnant" and disqualified.

## 87.

In May 2016, the Philadelphia Police Department (USA) admitted having disguised a surveillance SUV as a Google Maps car.

## 88.

Ribbon worms can eat themselves if there is no food.

### 89.

A US town (Woodland, North Carolina) rejected a solar farm project. They were worried it would "suck up all the energy from the Sun".

### 90.

In Jatinga, India, a strange and unexplained phenomenon happens each evening in the period from September to November. Hundreds of birds descend from the sky crashing into buildings and trees to their death.

### 91.

In Albania, thousands of people do not leave home being afraid of vendetta.

### 92.

Operation CHASE (an acronym for "Cut Holes And Sink 'Em") was a US Department of Defence program for the disposal of unwanted munitions at sea from May 1964 until the early 1970s. Some of the sinkings involved chemical weapons.

### 93.

In 2014, a Spanish village was renamed to Castrillo Mota de Judíos. The old name was Castrillo Matajudíos (Spanish for "Camp Kill the Jews").

## 94.

The newly elected Pope has his testicles inspected by cardinals. They are determined not to elect a female Pope again.

## 95.

Each year, around one hundred journalists get killed on duty worldwide.

## 96.

In 1930, George Stathakis survived his trip over Niagara Falls in a barrel. After the fall however, the barrel got trapped for almost one day behind a curtain of water and he died of suffocation. His pet turtle went along with him and survived.

## 97.

In 1998, the website of McDonald's (aimed mostly at children) stated that "Ronald McDonald is the absolute authority in everything".

## 98.

In Burgas, Bulgaria, there is a monument dedicated to the Soviet soldiers who died there in 1944. They did not fall in combat but after drinking methylated spirits.

99.

In 80% of the mass shootings in the USA, the killers had obtained their weapons legally.

100.

Europe-wide, Sweden has the highest rate per capita of reported rapes.

101.

Public dissection used to be a common practice in medieval Europe. In 1751, the UK Murder Act stipulated that all murderers be dissected after execution – a very strong deterrent as it was seen as the ultimate indignity.

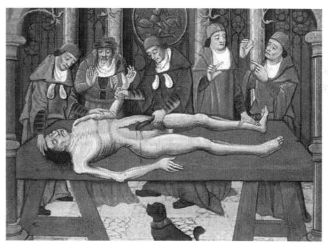

## 102.

In 2011, a motorcyclist, Philip A. Contos, was participating in an anti-helmet rally in Onondaga, New York (USA). He died after falling off his motorbike and hitting his head on the pavement. According to the police, a helmet could have saved his life.

## 103.

In 1980, Troy Leon Gregg, a convicted murderer in Georgia, USA, escaped from the prison the night before his execution. He was beaten to death in a bar fight later that night.

## 104.

In May 2016, a seven-year-old Japanese boy went missing after his parents left him for a while in the woods as punishment. He was found safe and sound a week later.

## 105.

In 2016, Facebook's Marketplace debut was very controversial with people trying to sell weird stuff. For instance, in London, UK, someone tried to "sell" his pregnant girlfriend for $400.

## 106.

The odds of getting struck by a lightning are a lot higher for men than for women.

### 107.

In 2016, the famous economist, Guido Menzio, was ethnically profiled and interrogated for hours in Philadelphia, USA, for... doing math on an American Airlines flight. A fellow passenger misread his differential equations scribbles for Arabic and reported him to the stewardess.

### 108.

According to the International Labour Organization, more people died of work-related accidents than in wars or natural disasters during the last few decades.

### 109.

The notorious prison of San Quentin in California, USA, has the largest death row in the Western Hemisphere.

### 110.

In 1838, the state of Missouri, USA, entered into a full-scale war against the Mormons, forcing them to leave the state. These events are also known as "1838 Mormon War".

### 111.

In the USA, garbage collectors die more often at work than police officers.

### 112.

Traffic accidents are one of the leading causes of death for US police officers.

### 113.

In most US states, it is still allowed to have a tiger as a pet.

### 114.

In 2002, fifteen girls burned to death inside their school in Mecca, Saudi Arabia. The religious police (aka mutaween) did not allow them to leave the burning building because the girls were not covering their hair.

### 115.

In talks with US top envoy Henry Kissinger in 1973, the Chinese leader Mao Zedong proposed to export millions of women to the United States. According to him, China was a "very poor country" and "what we have in excess is women."

### 116.

In July 2016, a Chinese tourist mistakenly applied for asylum in Germany when he actually wanted to report a theft. Without protest, he spent twelve days sleeping on a camping bed in a refugee centre before the mistake was revealed.

117.

During the Cold War, and more precisely in the period 1953 - 1976, beams of microwaves of 2.5 to 4.0 GHz were aimed at the US embassy building in Moscow, Russia. The sources were located in a neighbouring apartment building. Those microwaves might have been used to remotely charge the batteries of the microphones concealed in the building.

118.

During World War I, nine villages were totally obliterated around Verdun, France. They have remained uninhabited for more than a century now, but administratively they are alive: there are mayors appointed and occasionally ceremonies such as marriages and baptisms are still taking place.

119.

In 2009, an expert in kidnapping prevention, Felix Batista, was kidnapped in Saltillo, Mexico. Ironically, he had travelled there to give lectures on how to avoid kidnapping.

120.

Today, children who are adopted from abroad by US citizens automatically receive citizenship. However, between the 1950s and the 1980s more than 100,000 international adoptees were never naturalised.

## 121.

One third of the planet's food goes to waste. If food waste were a country, it would be the third largest producer of greenhouse gases in the world, only surpassed by the USA and China.

## 122.

In the 1950s, the only thing people in the United States of America feared more than polio was a nuclear war.

## 123.

In 1993, Garry Hoy threw himself over a glass wall on the 24th floor of the TD Centre in Toronto, Canada, and fell to his death when the window frame gave way. He was trying to prove to a group of visitors that the glass in his office was unbreakable.

## 124.

In 2016, Italy's Supreme Court ruled that masturbation in public was not a criminal offence as "the act was not included in the law as a crime".

## 125.

Until 1948, the non-alcoholic beverage 7 Up contained lithium citrate, a mood-stabilising drug.

126.

The Sedlec Ossuary is a small Roman Catholic chapel in the Czech Republic. It is estimated to contain the skeletons of up to 70,000 people, whose bones have been artistically arranged to form furnishings and decorations.

127.

In 1995, the American Sonny Graham received a heart transplant from a suicide victim. In 2004, he married his donor's widow. In 2008, Sonny killed himself in the same manner his donor did.

128.

Some grey seals are cannibals.

### 129.

In the 1990s, thousands of blood donors in the Henan province, China, contracted HIV due to poor medical safety practices. Donors' blood was pooled together, the plasma removed and the remaining cross-contaminated substance was injected back into the donors.

### 130.

In late 2016, a Japanese theme park froze 5000 fish under its ice rink in a bid to attract skaters. Instead, it appalled virtually everyone and the management had to shut the park down and apologise.

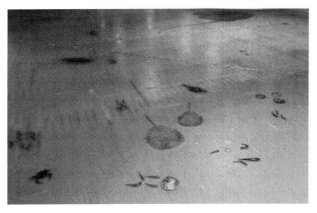

### 131.

The company Nike pays more money to Michael Jordan than to all its workers in Malaysia combined.

## 132.

In 2015, a top Saudi cleric issued a bizarre fatwa (a ruling on a point of Islamic law given by a recognised authority) allowing men to eat their own wives in case they feel extremely hungry.

## 133.

For qualifying for the United States Department of Agriculture's highest grade, the tomato ketchup has to contain no more than 30 fruit fly eggs per 100 grams (3.5 ounces).

## 134.

Are you an atheist? If so, it turns out that you are also considered a terrorist in Saudi Arabia and could be given a death sentence.

## 135.

Saudi Arabia banned Pokémon cards because of fears that the game encouraged Zionism. Do not ask me how exactly…

## 136.

Valentine's Day is outlawed in Saudi Arabia for religious reasons and all roses are seized.

## 137.

In July 1975, Erskine Ebbin was riding his moped when he was hit and killed by a taxi in Hamilton, Bermuda. The same taxi driver, carrying the same passenger, had killed Erskine's brother, Neville, in July the previous year. Both brothers were seventeen years old when they died, and had been using the same moped.

## 138.

On 1 April 2001, the waitresses in a restaurant in Florida, USA, were promised that whoever sold the most beer in the forthcoming month, would win a new Toyota. Some Jodee Berry won, but instead of a car, she was given a "toy Yoda" (the Star Wars character). She proceeded to sue and settled for an undisclosed amount.

Associated Press

**Jodee Berry of Panama City, Fla.**, sits with her toy Yoda at her lawyer's office Wednesday. Berry, a former Hooters waitress, has sued the restaurant where she worked saying she was promised a new Toyota for winning a beer sales contest in April. Berry, 26, believed that she had won a new car, but she was blindfolded, led to the parking lot and presented a toy Yoda, the little green guy from Star Wars.

### 139.

In North Korea, the victims have the right to kill their rapist. The person who was sexually assaulted can be one of the shooters in the firing squad during the execution.

### 140.

The Welsh comedian Tommy Cooper died of a heart attack on live television in 1984. The audience thought that it was part of the performance and continued applauding.

### 141.

Larry Rutman from Kentucky, USA, sued himself for 300,000 dollars after he threw a boomerang and it ended up knocking him on the head. He won the case and his insurance company paid the full amount.

### 142.

In 1977, Milo Stephens attempted to commit suicide by jumping in front of an oncoming subway train in New York City, USA. He survived and proceeded to sue the New York Transit Authority for negligence, winning a USD 650,000 settlement in 1983.

### 143.

Worldwide, millions of people own a mobile phone but not a toothbrush.

### 144.

In 1937, a baby fell down from a fourth-floor window and landed on Joseph Figlock who was passing by the street below in Detroit, Michigan (USA). They both survived. A year later, the same toddler fell from the same height on the same man. They both survived again.

### 145.

The Scottish surgeon, Robert Liston, performed an operation with a 300% mortality rate. While amputating a leg, he accidentally cut his assistant's fingers. Both the patient and the assistant succumbed from infection and a man in the audience died from a heart attack.

### 146.

The Soviet dictator, Joseph Stalin, and Sergei Prokofiev, one of the greatest composers of the 20th century, both died on 5 March 1953. As everyone in the USSR was obliged to mourn Stalin, it was impossible to transport Prokofiev's body to the funeral service for three full days.

### 147.

Australia's most dangerous creature is... the horse. Horses kill more people than all venomous animals combined do.

### 148.
Islam is the most widely-followed religion in Malaysia, but large minorities follow other faiths, including Christianity. In 2007, a court ruled that non-Muslims (and Christians in particular) could not use the word "Allah" although it is the Malay or Bahasa word for "God".

### 149.
In 2016, the Afghan Vice President, Abdul Rashid Dostum, kidnapped a rival politician, Ahmad Eshchi, a former governor of the Jowzjan province. For five days, the victim was subjected to false imprisonment, torture and sexual abuse.

### 150.
In 1849, the Hungarians pledged to refrain from clinking glasses for a period of 150 years and many of them still respect the pledge. After the failed Revolution of 1848, the Austrian generals executed thirteen of the Hungarian leaders and celebrated the victory by smugly clinking glasses.

### 151.
The shipping company that operated the Titanic stopped paying salaries to crew members from the day of sinking.

### 152.

Tribes in New Guinea only stopped the ritual
cannibalism in the 1950s.

### 153.

The youngest person to be sentenced to death in the
United States of America was an African-American
boy, George Stinney Jr. He was executed in 1944, at
the age of 14 years.

### 154.

In 2004, US officials announced that they would shoot
down any of the European Galileo navigation satellites
should it be considered a threat to
the US national security.

### 155.

In 1990, a 15-year-old girl, Nayirah, posed as an eyewitness and described the situation in Kuwait before the US Congress. Her testimony was widely publicised and influenced the US decision to attack Iraq. In fact, she was a daughter of the Kuwaiti ambassador to the USA and her story had been totally made up.

### 156.

Initially, chainsaws were developed as a tool for cutting bones during operations.

### 157.

In 2013, Russia convicted the lawyer Sergei Magnitsky in a posthumous trial. He had already died in prison in 2009 in suspicious circumstances.

### 158.

In late 2016, some twenty people died in southern Libya during four days of clashes between rival factions. It all started when a monkey belonging to one tribe attacked a child from the other camp.

### 159.

In the USA, the student loan debt is about 1.3 trillion dollars (as of 2017).

160.

In 2016, the first ever all-female pilot crew of
Royal Brunei Airlines landed in Saudi Arabia:
a country where women are not allowed to drive, but
can obtain a pilot's licence.

161.

In 1932, the US Public Health Service began a study
called the "Tuskegee Study of Untreated Syphilis in
the Negro Male". In the course of the study which
dragged for over forty years, 600 participants were
not given penicillin even after it became the drug of
choice for treating syphilis in 1947.

### 162.

The English custom "wife selling" meant exactly this: a husband could sell his wife. This weird tradition died out towards the end of the 19th century.

### 163.

Martha's Vineyard is an island off the coast of Massachusetts, USA. In the period 1700-1950, due to a recessive hereditary trait, some 5% of its population were born deaf.

### 164.

In Burundi, jogging is a crime. There are people in prison with long sentences, accused of using jogging as a cover for subversion.

### 165.

In 1927, general elections were held in Liberia. They entered the Guinness Book of Records as the most fraudulent ever. There were fewer than 15,000 registered voters, but one of the candidates received 243,000 votes.

### 166.

The United Nations acknowledged their involvement in the outbreak of the cholera epidemic in Haiti that killed thousands. The epidemic started in late 2010 near a UN base housing Nepalese peacekeepers.

### 167.

In 1990, a wave of so-called genitalia theft spread through Nigeria. The "victims" would claim that they felt a burning sensation when an unlucky stranger bumped into them "to steal their penis or to substitute it with a ghost-penis". The mass hysteria led to the murders of many innocent people by angry mobs.

### 168.

In the movie The Godfather, Vito Corleone (portrayed by Marlon Brando) had a son who almost killed his brother-in-law for beating his sister. In real life, Marlon Brando's son Christian killed the abusive boyfriend of his half-sister Cheyenne.

### 169.

Luo tribes of Kenya and Tanzania used to have a cruel tradition regarding single mothers who wanted to get married. The prospective husband had the right to request all step-children dead before the wedding.

### 170.

In February 2017, a Uruguayan court allowed a father to protect his unborn child and controversially prohibited the 8 weeks pregnant mother an abortion. Abortions are legal up until 12 weeks in this country.

## 171.

The Kielce Pogrom was the deadliest attack against Polish Jews after World War II. On 4 July 1946, Polish soldiers, police officers, and civilians killed forty-two Jews in Kielce, Poland.

## 172.

In 1898, a British officer named James Squid was stationed in modern-day Pakistan. In a state of drunkenness, he thought that a tree was moving towards him and ordered its arrest. The tree is still in chains.

## 173.

Homeowners in Colorado, USA, are only allowed to collect precipitation from their rooftops using no more than two rain barrels, with a combined maximum capacity of 0.416 m³ (110 gallons).

### 174.

In 2016, the pharmaceutical company Pfizer stopped selling to the US government drugs for use in lethal injections.

### 175.

In 2016, a state-owned TV aired a tutorial explaining how Moroccan women could cover with make-up the marks of domestic violence.

### 176.

In early 2017, China outlawed long beards and full-face coverings in the remote western region of Xinjiang as a part of its "anti-extremism" campaign.

### 177.

The following trademarks are registered today in the US: *Take Yo Panties Off* clothing; *Dangerous Negro* shirts; *Midget-Man* condoms and inflatable sex dolls; *Party With Sluts*; *Redneck Army* apparel; *Booty Call* sex aids; *Dumb Blonde* hair products.

### 178.

When the Spanish Civil War started in 1936, Spain had the world's fourth largest reserves of gold. Two-thirds of them were shipped to the USSR in exchange of military supplies.

### 179.

In 2013, two drunken Russian tourists attacked a bear at a zoo in Poland and beat the hell out of the poor animal. They thought it was a man in disguise.

### 180.

In 1918, the Great Influenza Pandemic killed up to 100 million people worldwide. It was called Spanish Flu as the Spanish press was free to report the real death toll while the other countries suppressed the numbers.

### 181.

In 1917, the UK government prohibited the use of rice at weddings and feeding of pigeons, due to food shortages.

### 182.

Before the invention of the gas mask, the only effective protection against gas attacks was a cloth soaked in human urine.

### 183.

In the period 1939-1940, the Soviet Union (USSR) occupied half of Poland, the three Baltic states (Lithuania, Latvia and Estonia), and invaded Finland. The League of Nations excluded the USSR in 1939; the USSR founded the United Nations six years later.

184.

"Kamikaze" means "divine wind". Japanese referred to an event from their history when a storm destroyed the entire fleet of the enemy. The kamikaze tactic was suggested in October 1944 in an attempt to balance the technological advantage of the invading American forces. Almost 4,000 kamikaze pilots died, sinking some fifty US ships.

185.

Only one in five Soviet men born in 1923 survived World War II.

186.

Stalin knew in advance about the upcoming Pearl Harbor attack and correctly concluded that Japan was not planning to attack the USSR. This enabled him to safely withdraw numerous divisions from Siberia and launch the first Soviet counter-offensive against the Germans one day before the Japanese attack on Pearl Harbor.

187.

The Nazi regime in Germany used punch cards provided by European subsidiaries of IBM to sort out people destined for concentration camps.

188.

In Normandy, the Allies captured several Asians in German uniforms shortly after the D-Day. One of them was Yang Kyoungjong, a Korean soldier who is to date the only soldier to fight on three sides of a war. He was first conscripted into the Imperial Japanese Army. Then he was captured by the Soviet troops in Manchuria and forced into the Soviet Red Army. In turn, the German Wehrmacht captured him in Ukraine and pressed him into fighting for Germany.

189.

The British Prime Minister, Winston Churchill, endorsed in 1945 a plan named "Operation Unthinkable". In short, it was about invading the Soviet Union in a surprise attack, right after the end of WWII.

190.

In 1939, the London Zoo, UK, killed all their venomous animals. They feared that the animals might escape during a bombing.

191.

In the period 1942-1945, the number of US citizens kept by the US government in internment camps on US soil was higher than the number of all US prisoners of war in Japanese camps combined.

## 192.

In 1938, Time magazine pronounced Adolf Hitler the man of the year. In 1942: Joseph Stalin.

## 193.

On 12 September 1942, in what is known as the *Laconia incident*, a German submarine torpedoed a British troopship and then started rescuing the survivors. Equipped with a red cross and sending open radio signals to the Allies, the submarine had its deck packed with rescued people when a US bomber deliberately attacked, killing many of them. The bomber's crew were then awarded medals for bravery.

## 194.

In the United States of America, zebras hurt more zookeepers than tigers do.

195.
During WWII, some German pilots intentionally ruptured their eardrums to prevent air pressure issues.

196.
The German city of Konstanz (at the German-Swiss border) was never bombed by the Allied Forces as it intentionally left all its lights on at night. Allied bombers thought it was a city in Switzerland.

197.
Although all powers possessed chemical weapons during WWII, only Japan (in China) and Italy (in Ethiopia) used them.

198.
The Japanese city of Nagasaki was not the initial target for the second A-bomb: it was Kokura, which had been covered in smog at the time. Nagasaki was the alternative target city.

199.
In early 2017, a joint study by the Leeds Beckett University (UK) and the University of Missouri (USA) found that religious countries are likely to perform worse in science and maths.

## 200.

In late 2017, Reuters announced the disturbing results of their investigation on the trade of human body parts in the USA. Their reporters were able to legally purchase from the company Restore Life numerous body parts, including "two human heads, each priced at $300".

## 201.

In 2004, Canada became the first country in the world to ban the sale and advertisement of baby walkers. The government decided to take this step after several fatal accidents.

## 202.

Out of the 105,000 German soldiers who surrendered at Stalingrad, Russia, just 5,500 came back home. The last German prisoners of war came back home only in 1955.

## 203.

In 2007, over 34,000 Americans committed suicide. No-one was killed by terrorists on US soil in the same year.

# CHAPTER III

*Facts about human and animal sexuality*

### 1.

Humans are one of the few primates who do not have a penis bone (*baculum*).

### 2.

Of all mammals, only humans, chimpanzees and dolphins form a coalition of male individuals to attack other males.

### 3.

When flatworms mate, two "males" fence one another with their bifurcated penises. The winner (the one that stabs the other with its penis) remains male while the loser becomes female.

4.

Male gorillas weigh up to four times more than male chimpanzees but have four-time smaller testicles.

5.

In 2006, in the former Upper Nile State of Sudan (today Republic of South Sudan), a man named Mr. Tombe was ordered by the council of elders to "marry" a goat named Rose, with which he was caught having sex. Additionally, Mr. Tombe had to pay a dowry equivalent of 50 US dollars to the goat's owner.

6.

The Netherlands recognise forced kissing as a sexual assault. The offender could face up to fifteen years in prison.

7.

The word "boobies" was first used in 1934 by Henry Miller.

8.

In 2016, a survey by the US online dating site Match.com found out that 39% of its users judged the suitability of the potential partners by their grammar.

9.

Hippos mate and give birth in the water.

## 10.

The mating behaviour of *Phasmatodea* (aka stick insects or stick-bugs) is impressive because of the surprisingly long duration of some pairings. For instance, the *Necroscia sparaxes*, found in India, remains coupled for up to 79 days at a time.

## 11.

In 2008, a study found out that men who masturbate more than twenty-one times per month have a lower chance of getting prostate cancer.

## 12.

In the period 2012-2015, a Hong Kong billionaire was offering up to 100 million dollars to any man who could "turn" his lesbian daughter straight.

## 13.

In 2014, UK's internet porn filter architect, Patrick Rock, was arrested for... child porn offences.

## 14.

The popular Australian ice cream chain, Ben and Jerry's, announced in May 2017 that they would not allow customers to purchase two scoops of the same flavour until Australia legalised gay marriages. Same-sex marriages were eventually legalised in December 2017.

### 15.
Male earwigs have penises longer than their bodies.

### 16.
Generally, humans have a better chance of finding a mate in densely populated areas. It is not at all that easy for the birds in big cities, however, because their seductive mating calls cannot be heard over traffic.

### 17.
At one moment, dictionaries were removed from classrooms in southern California, USA, after a parent complained about his child reading the definition of "oral sex".

### 18.
Viagra was originally designed to lower blood pressure. As a heart medicine it was a disappointment, but had a remarkable effect on men with erectile dysfunction.

### 19.
The Skoptsy were a secret sect in Russia in the period between the 1780s and the 1940s. They were best known for practicing castration of men and mastectomy (surgical removal of breasts) of women in line with their teachings against sexual lust.

### 20.

A medicine called Truvada can be successfully used as protection against HIV during sex without a condom.

### 21.

In 2016, Facebook's software blocked a photograph of a 16th-century statue of Neptune in Bologna, Italy, claiming it was "sexually explicit".

### 22.

The thinnest condom is just 0.036 mm (0.0014 in).

### 23.

After sexual intercourse, men's beards grow faster.

## 24.

Premarital sex is still illegal in several US states.

## 25.

In May 2016, the Indonesian police seized an inflatable sex doll from a remote village after its inhabitants and social media mistook it for an "angel" and started to worship it.

## 26.

Some female fireflies mimic the light signals of other firefly species to attract, kill, and eat the lured males.

## 27.

Walt Disney made a documentary named "A Few Quick Facts about Venereal Disease".

## 28.

Female Kangaroos have three vaginas.

# CHAPTER IV

*Myth vs. Fact*

1.
Slugs have four noses.

**Wrong:** a slug has four tentacles that perform sensory functions. A slug has **no** noses and it only uses two of the four tentacles to smell.

2.
Female co-workers synchronise menstruation (the so-called McClintock effect).

**It is a myth,** due to a flawed study performed by Ms McClintock in 1971.

3.

The inventor of 7 Up was an albino, and the red dot on the logo is supposed to represent his red eyes.

**It is an urban legend:** there are no official references to Mr Grigg having been an albino, and the 7 Up logo with the red dot came into use in the 1970s, after he had died.

4.

Bern is the capital of Switzerland.

**It is not precise:** Swiss law does not designate a capital city as such. The federal parliament and government are indeed located in Bern, but the federal courts are located in other cities.

5.

In Ancient Rome, a thumb up meant life and a thumb down meant death for the gladiator.

**It is a myth** and Hollywood movies got it totally wrong: a thumb up in fact meant death for the gladiator.

6.

Pineapple juice can erase your fingerprints.

**Not true:** pineapple juice can cause an unpleasant burning sensation on your skin and make your fingertips swell, but will not erase your fingerprints.

7.

Crabs have eight legs.

**Myth:** in fact, crabs have ten legs.

8.

House dust mostly comprises dead human skin.

**It is a myth:** we do shed dead skin cells but they constitute a tiny portion of the dust.

9.

Wait at least thirty minutes after eating before you swim!

**There is no evidence** that not respecting this advice could endanger your life. Most probably it was just parents wanting a 30-minute break to relax after a big lunch...

10.

French fries were invented by American soldiers stationed in Belgium during World War I.

**It is a myth:** the origins of the dish have been traced back to Belgium, where historians claim potatoes were being fried in the late 1600s.

### 11.
Mosquitoes' buzz is caused by their wings beating against the air.

**Wrong,** there is a specific organ at the base of the wings which makes the sound.

### 12.
Buffalo Bill killed many buffalos.

**It is a myth:** Buffalo Bill did not kill a single buffalo in his life; he killed however thousands of bison.

BUFFALO          BISON

## 13.

You will completely sink into and will drown if caught in quick sand.

**False:** people can sink deep into the soupy mixture while they struggle. However, its buoyancy makes it impossible for the human body to be completely submerged.

## 14.

Bears were named after the Arctic.

**It is exactly the opposite:** the Arctic was named after the bear. It was "the region of the bear", where bears lived ( *"arctos"* meaning "bear" in Ancient Greek).

## 15.

If you cross the Panama Canal from east to west, you will end up in the Pacific.

**Simply wrong:** the Atlantic entrance to the Panama Canal is farther west than the Pacific one.

16.
Centipedes have 100 legs.

**It is a myth:** not a single species of centipedes has exactly 100 legs. There is an easy way to differentiate centipedes and millipedes. Millipedes have two pairs of legs on the most body segments, while centipedes always have a single pair of legs per segment.

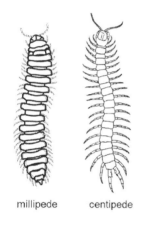

millipede     centipede

17.
Tigers roar before attack.

**Wrong:** tigers do not normally roar at other species. Instead, they roar to communicate with far-off tigers.

18.
Strict vegans can eat figs.

**Not really:** occasionally, a fig wasp enters a fig and dies there. The insect's body is afterwards partially or fully absorbed by the ripening fig.

19.
The City of London is part of London.

**Wrong:** despite these confusingly close names, the two Londons have separate city halls and elect separate mayors, who collect separate taxes to fund separate police who enforce separate laws.

20.
The term "Third World" is related to poverty.

**It is a myth:** it has nothing to do with poverty. "Third World" was referring to countries that were not aligned with either the Communist Soviet bloc or the NATO bloc during the Cold War.

21.

The upper and the lower door hinges are at the same distance from the top and the bottom end of the door respectively.

**They are normally not:** due to an optical illusion, they appear to be at the same distance from the top and the bottom.

22.

Being fat is bad for health.

**Partly true,** but being severely underweight is more dangerous for health than being obese.

23.

Sharks are the most dangerous thing that could kill you when at the beach.

**Not really:** more people die while digging a sand hole on the beach than by shark attacks.

24.
The shuttle Enterprise has never flown.

**Partially true:** Enterprise has never flown... in space.

25.
Atlas holds Earth on his shoulders.

**Most people get it wrong** – Atlas holds the sky and not Earth.

26.
Ferdinand Magellan was the first to circumnavigate Earth.

**It is a myth:** Ferdinand Magellan did not finish the circumnavigation of Earth, dying midway. It was his slave, Enrique De Malaca (aka "Henry the Black"), who did finish it. By the way, the latter is considered a hero in several countries in Southeast Asia.

27.
Violin strings are made of catgut.

**It is a myth:** violin strings are actually made of sheep or goat intestines, and not catgut.

28.
In the UK, you have to drive only on the left-hand side.

**Mostly true** but upon entering and leaving the Savoy Hotel in London, you drive on the only road in the United Kingdom with a right-hand movement.

29.
Most people in India are Buddhists.

**Actually,** Buddhism is the religion of only 0.7% of the Indian population, not making it in the top three.

30.
3D printers are a recent invention.

**In fact,** the first 3D printer was invented back in 1983.
Many of the underlying patents expired a couple of
years ago, making these devices more popular
and affordable.

31.
Many pirates were one-eyed.

**It is a myth:** historically, most pirates did not wear eye
bandage because of a missing or blind eye. They
simply wanted to be better prepared for a fight in the
darkness inside the ship they were trying to conquer
(by moving the patch to the other eye).

32.
Cows fart methane.

**Overstated:** cows actually burp most of the methane.
The quantity of gas from the other end is negligible.

## 33.

Turbot is born with two eyes on the top side.

**In fact,** turbot is born with one eye on each side of the body. With time, the body flattens and the eye from the bottom side moves to the top.

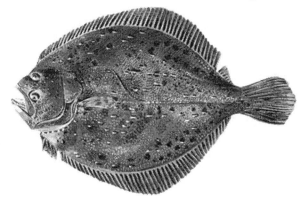

## 34.

QWERTY keyboard was deliberately set out that way to slow typists down. Going too fast would make the hammers in the old typewriter jam together.

**Widely spread, this claim has not been supported by any evidence.** For instance, the letters E and R are adjacent, while the combinations "er" and "re" are among the most common in English.

35.
Adult moths eat clothes.

**It is a myth:** to start with, the majority of the adult moths do not even have a mouth. It is the moth larvae that feed off of the keratin in your clothes.

36.
Raindrops have a "raindrop" shape.

**It is a myth:** most people are unaware that raindrops (and most liquids) have spherical form while they fall through air. Historically, shot ball towers used this knowledge to create close to perfect spheres (bullets) by dripping down the molten lead.

37.
Killer whales are a species of whales.

**Wrong:** killer whales, or orcas, are the largest of the dolphins and one of the world's most powerful predators.

38.
The Nazis invented the swastika.

**It is a myth:** the swastika is an ancient religious symbol, used in the temples in Egypt, Greece, China and India.

39.
A microwave oven uses most of the consumed electricity to heat food.

**This one is counterintuitive:** annually, a microwave oven would consume more electricity powering its digital clock rather than heating food.

40.
ODEON means "Oscar Deutsch Entertains Our Nation".

**False,** regardless of what Mr Deutsch was claiming.
It is an Ancient Greek word, meaning "a building used for musical performances".

At the very end, I am honourably mentioning the famous taxonomist, Carl Linnaeus.
In the 18th century, he debunked the existence of many mythical creatures, such as the hydra, the phoenix, and the satyr. Ironically, he also questioned the existence of one real animal, the shrinking frog.

###

# VERIFICATION PROCESS

To start with, however a great read Wikipedia is, I have never used it to confirm facts; I rather checked the sources listed there and evaluated them.

Anything science-related like *"The vast majority of modern people have in their DNA between 1% and 4% of Neanderthal DNA"* would need to be confirmed by at least two (preferably three) separate scientific publications, be it on paper or online of the sort of http://www.science.gov/, http://www.nasa.gov/, http://www.britannica.com/, http://www.sciencemag.org/, https://www.newscientist.com/, https://www.genome.gov/education/, http://www.howstuffworks.com/, http://www.merriam-webster.com/.

For events or facts of the type *"Norwegians use the word "Texas" as a synonym for "crazy"*, I checked at least three reputable newspaper articles and/or confirmed television reports. Example for newspapers/TV channels used to verify events: The New York Times, Washington Post, Wall Street Journal, The Guardian, The Economist, Financial Times, Times of India, Le Monde, The Sydney Morning Herald, Frankfurter Allgemeine Zeitung, Bloomberg, Al Jazeera, Reuters, Associated Press, BBC, TV5 MONDE, CNN, etc.

The scientific publications and websites of the best universities worldwide are also consistently checked (excerpt from the list): University of Cambridge, Stanford University, University of Oxford, California Institute of Technology, Massachusetts Institute of Technology, Harvard University, Princeton University, Imperial College London, ETH Zurich – Swiss Federal Institute of Technology, Yale University, Columbia University, University of Toronto, Humboldt University of Berlin, University of Tokyo, Heidelberg University, University of Melbourne, Peking University etc.

# ACKNOWLEDGEMENTS

This book is dedicated to my family: my loving wife Anna, my curious and restless sons Pavel and Nikolay, and my mother Maria, who sparked my interest in reading. Thank you for being so patient with me during the lengthy process of writing. You are my inspiration!

Many thanks to the editors Jonathon Tabet and Andrea Leitenberger; to all test readers, friends, and colleagues who provided vital feedback and constructive criticism.

I am truly impressed by the Kickstarter community, which not only was great in the crowdfunding part, but also provided guidance and shared precious experience.

## ZEALOUS TEST READERS:

Abdoulaye Faye
Agnes Bannink
Alexandra Oliveira-Jones
Alexandre Berger
Desi Morate
Gary Hammond
Heather Wilkinson
Kathy Tallentire
Kathy Tanghe
Laura Perkins
Lilian Dean Dodson
William Wilcock

I hope you have enjoyed this book. I would greatly appreciate it if you write your honest **review** on Amazon and/or on GoodReads.com

\*\*\*

You could also check out my other books and **DOWNLOAD A FREE SAMPLE** from my website RaiseYourBrain.com :

## 1123 Hard To Believe Facts

## Which Is NOT True? - The Quiz Book

## Fascinating Facts for the Whole Family
*(finalist from The Wishing Shelf Book Awards)*

You could also subscribe for my newsletter and learn first about my future projects.

You could also follow me on GoodReads: a great place for everyone who loves reading.

Nayden Kostov's Stats

★★★★⯪ 4.06 avg rating — 217 ratings

| | | | |
|---|---|---|---|
| number of works | 4 | added by unique users | 9,504 |
| total books added | 14,291 | followers | 206 |
| total ratings | 217 | friends | 55 |
| total reviews | 49 | books I've added | 176 |
| on to-read shelf | 13,811 | books I've reviewed | 26 |

View recent work stats »

YOUR BOOKS                                      Add a book

**1123 Hard to Believe Facts**
by Nayden Kostov
169 ratings (3.98 avg) · 34 text reviews
to-read: 8,067 people
currently-reading: 133 people
stats

**Which is not True?: The Quiz Bo...**
by Nayden Kostov
25 ratings (4.16 avg) · 7 text reviews
to-read: 4,297 people
currently-reading: 38 people
stats

**Fascinating Facts for the Whole...**
by Nayden Kostov
19 ratings (4.53 avg) · 5 text reviews
to-read: 1,443 people
currently-reading: 21 people

**853 Hard To Believe Facts**
by Nayden Kostov
5 ratings (4.80 avg) · 3 text reviews
to-read: 4 people
stats

# ABOUT THE AUTHOR

Born in Bulgaria, I have lived in places like Germany, Belgium and Iraq, before settling down with my family in Luxembourg. With varied interests, I have always suffered from an insatiable appetite for facts stemming from an unrestrainable intellectual curiosity. It has certainly influenced my academic background and career: after acquiring Master degrees in Greek Philology, German and English Translation, I graduated in Crisis Management and Diplomacy and, most recently, undertook an MBA.

My career has been equally broad and diverse, swinging from that of an army paratrooper and a military intelligence analyst; through to that of a civil servant with the European Commission, and presently, that of a clerk, performing purely financial tasks in a major bank.

Member of MENSA.

# CONNECT WITH THE AUTHOR

Email: n.kostov@raiseyourbrain.com

Facebook: www.facebook.com/raiseyourbrain/

Twitter: @RaiseYourBrain

Blog: www.RaiseYourBrain.com

OTHER BOOKS AVAILABLE ON AMAZON:

1123 Hard To Believe Facts
Which Is NOT True? - The Quiz Book
Fascinating Facts for the Whole Family

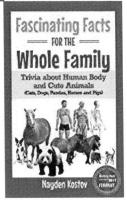

Printed in Great Britain
by Amazon